Communication
Means Talking
Together

How You Can Inspire Your Team
and Lead with Purpose

ARJUN BUXI

Archway Publishing books may be ordered through booksellers or by contacting:

Archway Publishing
1663 Liberty Drive
Bloomington, IN 47403
www.archwaypublishing.com
844-669-3957

ISBN: 978-1-6657-0659-9 (sc)
ISBN: 978-1-6657-0658-2 (hc)
ISBN: 978-1-6657-0660-5 (e)

Library of Congress Control Number: 2021908617

Print information available on the last page.

Archway Publishing rev. date: 06/28/2021

Contents

Introduction

Dear reader, thank you for choosing this book.

I wrote this book for current and aspiring leaders in all industries—for-profit businesses, nonprofit organizations, and all other walks of life—who sometimes struggle to find their voices, make an impact, and be respected by others.

Like a lot of people, I grew up wanting to help others, and the spirit of this book is to give any human being the chance to be courageous and influential in their life.

What is communication?

Think of an argument you may have had with someone, especially someone you might care about. Heated words like "You don't understand me" and "I don't know what you want" and all manner of curses are exchanged—contributing to a feeling of friction.

Very unpleasant, right?

On the most elemental level, in our deepest heart of hearts, our souls, we want to be heard, understood, acknowledged, and appreciated. And sometimes that doesn't mean the other person likes us or agrees with us or changes their mind, but at least that person knows where we stand on the issue, and then the antagonistic feeling that was playing out between us subsides, and our relationship can continue.

That is communication. The process of building, defining, and furthering community.

Communication is talking, together.

There's no communication without sharing and togetherness, even if it's just between two people.

Together we create ideas, meanings, processes, knowledge, and most of all, value.

Talking together drives families, societies, economies, countries, and the world.

We talk in real time (synchronous communication) or leave messages and emails for each other to read later (asynchronous communication).

We write, we speak, and we send images, gifs, videos, links, and emojis.

The medium—spoken, written, or visual —doesn't matter. All that matters is that the other person *gets it*. So long as there is some meaning, there is communication. So long as there is sharing in the process, there is communication.

Communication is about choices, goals, and purposes.

I've always been fascinated by people and *how* they interact, *why* they interact, and with *whom* they choose to interact.

That's really it, right? The choices we make and the rational and emotional drivers behind those choices. It's probably fair to say that we act just as much on the rational or logical side as we do on the emotional side of things.

As soon as we start making decisions, no matter our titles or stations, we become leaders.

Communication is inseparable from culture and leadership.

In my consulting and college professorship work, I work with clients and students alike to create well-rounded, vibrant people who can lead. People who use powerful communication skills to execute leadership goals and build a great culture among their teams.

I know others teach communication, culture, and leadership separately. Whenever I begin working with someone, I find that person to be full of doubts, fears, and concerns of different kinds. Thus, it is essential to teach leaders to speak well and with courage, and show them how to tell their stories and make a persuasive argument. Then, once they're standing on their own two feet, they begin the hard work in building their leadership personas, their teams, and their organizations.

I have found that one must first learn to speak. Only then can one lead.

That is essentially the order in which this book is written.

Respect, logic, and connection.

The ancient Greeks wrote the terms *ethos, pathos,* and *logos*, which make up the combination of a speaker's presence or persona, the emotional tone, and the evidence-based arguments that drive home any point we're trying to communicate.

My *ethos* is that I gave my first public speech in fifth grade with zero preparation in front of a thousand children and the school principal, and I never looked back.

After that followed hundreds of public speeches and debates over decades. I captained many winning school debate teams, got a master's degree in communication, and taught communication at universities.

The skills of oratory, argumentation, persuasion, and interpersonal communication transfer seamlessly from the stage to the boardroom. I have trained executives and corporate leaders, making my mark in Silicon Valley.

I only tell you this to demonstrate that I know what I'm talking about.

The *logos* of this book is that communication and leadership are the key cross-industry skills demanded by employers and schools alike, so if you're trying to make your mark in hypercompetitive schools and corporations with sharp communication and leadership skills, *but don't know how to move forward*, this is the right book for you.

The *pathos* of this book is that I'd love to have a ten-chapter conversation with you, arranged in two parts—communication and leadership—about making your mark as a leader with radically improved communication skills.

The chapters address ten topics that I think will remove your fears, open your mind, and give you both food for thought and tools for success.

These ten topics will make you an excellent communicator, a perceptive thinker, an inspiring leader, and really, in the end, a wonderful person.

So in short, let's talk. Together.

PART 1

COMMUNICATION

1

COMMUNICATION ANXIETY

So you're in the office, and you're supposed to be making a presentation.

The grip is strong. Words fail you. All eyes are on you.

And your mind goes blank.

When will this nightmare end?

The cliché goes that we in the United States fear public speaking right up there alongside death and poisonous snakes.

What if I told you it wasn't just a cliché but a statistic?[1]

While not everyone speaks to packed stadiums or large audiences, most people in the workplace find themselves frequently making presentations to groups of five to ten people, if not more.

And what's more, if the group is small, the stakes are frequently quite high, not just in terms of money but also reputation. So it is not surprising that this leads to a lot of anxiety.

These communication situations, while not in large groups, still qualify as public speaking situations. *Public speaking*, after all, is about speaking in a somewhat more structured, scripted, or formal way than normal conversation to a group of about five or more people.

---

[1] Geoffrey Brewer, "Snakes Top List of Americans' Fears," *Gallup News Service,* March 19, 2001, https://news.gallup.com/poll/1891/snakes-top-list-americans-fears.aspx.

Before we can really get into the key skills of communication and leadership, we have to address this speaking anxiety that many of us experience, what it means, and how we can overcome it.

✍ The Nature of This Anxiety

When we are in a speaking situation, a rush of self-doubting questions assail us:

- What if I forget my words?
- What if they don't agree with me?
- Why are they looking at me?
- Is this really worth it?

This is self-catastrophizing[2]—an inner monologue in our minds that is imagining with increasing intensity (leading up to a crescendo) the vast array of things that can go wrong and just how wrong they can go.

This can even manifest itself physically. People have been known to go blank, shake, drop note cards, stutter, stammer, ramble, stumble over words, lose their place in notes, and more.

✍ How to Manage Speaking Anxiety

Being a great communicator requires, at a minimum, two things: focusing on the needs of the audience and understanding how you can fulfill those needs.

With Maslow's hierarchy, it is good to remember that your audience needs to feel that they are achieving meaning and higher potential in their lives by helping others and contributing to society through their projects or work.

So when preparing your speech, first prepare for the audience.

---

[2] Alice Boyes, "What is Catastrophizing?" *In Practice* (blog), *Psychology Today*, January 10, 2013, https://www.psychologytoday.com/us/blog/in-practice/201301/what-is-catastrophizing-cognitive-distortions.

Give them good content in a memorable way that achieves their highest goals.

Put yourself in their shoes for a moment. What would *you* want if you were in the audience?

Let me make a few guesses:

- ☐ You'd like to learn something new so that you feel your time was well spent.
- ☐ You'd like to be entertained a bit, even if that's not the main goal.
- ☐ You'd like the speaker to speak honestly and respect your intelligence.
- ☐ You'd like the speaker to be knowledgeable about their topic or an expert
- ☐ You'd like the speaker to be trustworthy and likeable.

In short, you want to have a good time!

If I follow the above rules, is there room for the audience to actively dislike me?

Unless I go out of my way to insult people, question their intelligence, make antisocial statements or prejudiced remarks, or anything like that, I'm starting on good footing.

Then come my ethical goals: first, to *speak truthfully on topics I know about* in a way that is helpful to my audience and secondly, to avoid manipulative tactics.

Here's the secret: no matter what they say, remember that *the audience secretly admires you for getting up in front of people and speaking.* It's scary for them too! Especially if they know you personally.

The good people will let you know how much they respect you. The others? In time, you will win them over too with a strong message that inspires them and by speaking with self-belief.

FEARLESS PUBLIC SPEAKING

**SPEAK TRUTHFULLY
ON TOPICS YOU
KNOW ABOUT**

**SPEAK FROM PREPARED
IDEAS, NOT A PREPARED
SCRIPT**

**HAVE A SIMPLE AND
CLEAR LOGIC**

**BEGINNING, MIDDLE AND
END**

CATCHY OPEN AND CLOSE

**HAVE EMPATHY FOR
YOURSELF**

**AUDIENCE IS ROOTING FOR
YOU**

**BELIEVE YOUR MESSAGE,
BECOME THE MESSAGE**

Figure 1. Tips to speak without fear

How to Prepare and Not Get Anxious

1. *Pick the right speech format.*

Here's the key: don't try to memorize the speech word-for-word. That will only add to the pressure.

There are multiple kinds of speaking formats. Here are just a few:

- *Memorized speaking* is when we have written out and learned by heart the script for our speaking situation. An application of this today is movies or TV shows, where actors must know their dialogues before filming.

- *Scripted speaking*, or manuscript style, is when one has a script but instead of memorizing, one reads it out verbatim. A reason for doing this is to get it just right per the author's needs or for legal reasons, since a single out-of-place word can change the meaning of a legal document. These days, many public figures or news anchors use teleprompters that have the script of the show or speech on a screen, and they read it aloud word-for-word.
- *Impromptu speaking* is when we speak "off the cuff" (more detail on this in chapter 4). This categorizes many daily situations, but more structured environments also need impromptu speaking, such as job interviews, panel discussions, classroom discussions, brainstorming meetings, and so on.
- *Extemporaneous speaking* is when we speak from a set of prepared *ideas* rather than a set script. You know how people like it when we seem real and speak from the heart? That's what we're aiming for, at least the audience's experience of it.

Extemporaneous style is the one recommended for most situations since it blends the strongest aspects of all speaking styles: semiprepared and well-structured content with a semispontaneous, natural-sounding delivery.

The best speaking is like the best makeup: you prepare so that it looks unprepared and natural.

2. *Get the sequence of your ideas together.*

Structure, content, and delivery are the three keys of any good speech or presentation. Like the pillars of a house, if even one of them is weak or—worse—missing altogether, the house falls.

Bottom line, there's no point in you having the best-sounding voice, the most important message, or even the greatest arguments if your audience can't follow along.

Let's do an overview of what a clear and simple speech structure might look like.

First among the ingredients for a good speech is the *introduction*. Start with a question, interesting factoid, or topic-relevant joke to get your audience's attention and set the stage. Then tell us why this topic is important. Next are the *three key ideas* that you frame under a banner or *thesis*, as well as a *preview* or snapshot of those three key ideas before you begin. For example, "Today we'll talk about how growing revenue is more important than saving costs. We'll also talk about why growth is the biggest predictor of company success, how to manage costs without hampering growth, and how to measure both of these."

Go through each idea patiently and with some redundancy for the sake of your audience's memory. Then *summarize* what you went over, and end with a powerful *closing line*.

In chapter 2, we'll delve into the intricacies of speech structure and how to expertly keep your audience engaged throughout.

3. *Frame preemptive audience questions and "talk it out."*

This is a technique I use to engage and pivot at the same time. You want to prepare a few questions ahead of time. To do that, put yourself in the shoes of the audience and wonder, *What points of disagreement might the audience have with my views?* Think up at least three such points and write down simple, straightforward, nondefensive responses.

> You might say: "So we have an impossible choice here ... Do we cancel an order with one of our best customers or risk sending a product that might ruin our reputation?" And as it did to me, it may occur to you ... "Customers are hard to find, yes, but the good ones will always understand, even if they take a while to get back to the relationship you once had. But a bad product, a bad brand? That stinks forever."

4. *Pick out some key phrases that work, are worth repeating, and really convey how you feel about the topic.*

Every speech has some key words or phrases that really stick in your head and frame the speech's purpose and meaning. "Ask what you can do for your country ..." "We hold these truths to be self-evident ..." "I have a dream ..." They stand out from the rest of the speech and might, in some cases, be a perfect summary for the speech and its main point.

How can you pick a perfect branding or memorable line? Keep in eye out for the chiasmus and rhyming.

A *chiasmus* is a line composed of two clauses in which the second clause is the inversion of the first. Its goal is to make the audience reframe the topic being discussed and look at it from a new perspective. Famous examples include Mark Twain's "It's not the size of the dog in the fight, it's the size of the fight in the dog" and, of course, President Kennedy's "Ask not what your country can do for you, ask what *you* can do for your country."

As for *rhyming*, let's face it, ad jingles stick in our heads better than anything, as do most popular songs. Keep it optimistic, future oriented, and unifying.

A great example is from a speech in the 1996 Hollywood blockbuster *Independence Day*. Right before the final charge of the humans against the extraterrestrial armies, actor Bill Pullman, who played the US president, gave a speech that included the lines, "We will not go quietly into the night. We will not vanish without a fight!"

Though part of a longer speech, these lines still ring loudly decades later because they match up in cadence, simplicity, and of course rhyming. The pronoun "we" signifies unity. It is talking about preserving the human race from an external threat and hence is future oriented and optimistic.

✎ Closing Thoughts

Yes, it is sometimes scary to address a group of people.

Leaders are constantly faced with this: the group of faces looking at you for answers, and yet there is doubt lurking within you.

But what if you are the person in this moment who has the right message, the right demeanor, the right kind of reassurance that everyone desperately needs?

Exigence is a word in rhetoric that approximately means "the critical situation or emergency demanding a written or spoken response."[3]

The best way to understand it is a phrase we often use: "somebody needed to say it."

Indeed! And why shouldn't that person be you?

Finally, to be a great communicator, you must truly *believe* your message. You must *become one with* your message.

By uniting with your message and practicing what you preach, you can truly advocate for even the most unpopular idea.

If you preach that "we will make the decision based on data," then find compelling data and link it to each decision.

If you believe that "our company is a family," use your speech to recognize the great contributors of your team and make sure praise isn't sparse.

Lastly, to unite with your message, you must embrace the *risk* of communication.

Think not of the anxiety, the failure, and the judgment that *might* come your way; instead think of how many small, great surprises await you.

There are no guarantees that the decision you make is the perfect one. Just the best one.

So go out there and speak your mind.

---

[3] Richard Nordquist, "Exigence in Rhetoric," *Thoughtco,* last updated July 16, 2019, https://www.thoughtco.com/exigence-rhetoric-term-1690688.

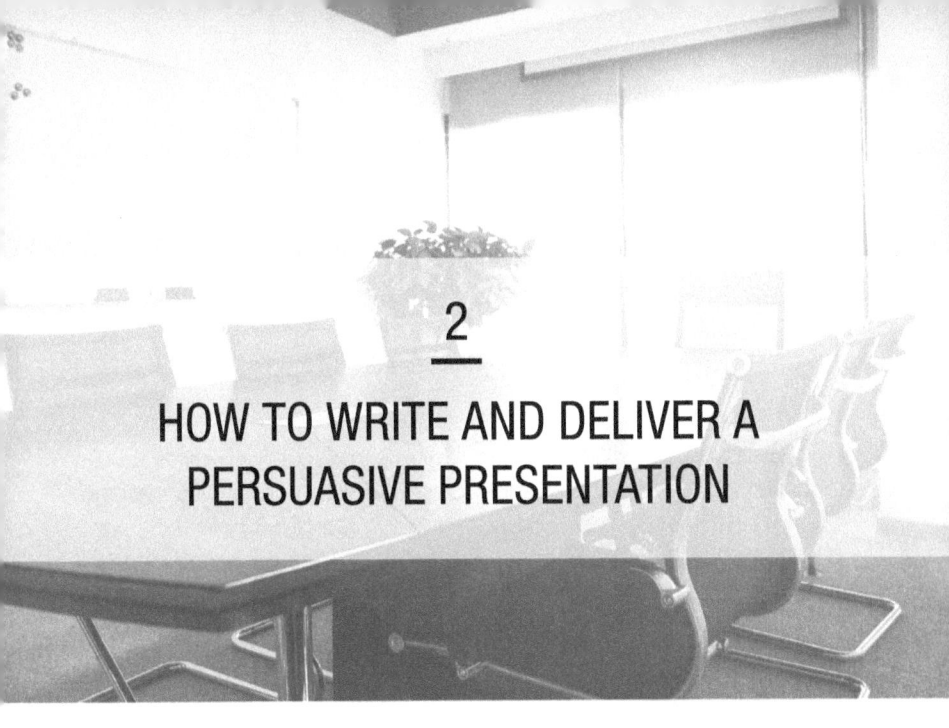

2

HOW TO WRITE AND DELIVER A PERSUASIVE PRESENTATION

In this chapter, we move from talking about speaking anxiety and how to overcome it, to preparing for a high-pressure speaking situation in which we have to persuade our audience to agree with us.

So I'm looking down, reviewing my scrappy notes for my speech tonight, scribbled on a Starbucks napkin. The perfect narrative symphony I had imagined is now a patchy cloudscape of ideas. None of which last more than thirty seconds.

Uh-oh.

Most of us don't memorize speeches anymore. US audiences find this style less "real" and not "natural," so they can't relate to us. We always get advice about "speaking from the heart," and again, that's good up to a point.

High-pressure speeches are defined by a low(er) margin for error coupled with a high-stakes outcome. In other words, you have a lot to lose or gain and not much opportunity for do-overs. In the corporate environment, such presentations may include the approval of budgets for big projects like purchasing of new software or equipment that is crucial for operations but comes with a hefty price tag. How can I convince management I've done my homework and that the investment is worth it?

So, why not just, like, talk?

Fair point, but what if you needed to

- State complex information,
- Stick to some choice key phrases (for legal/stylistic reasons), or
- Meet a time limit?

Scribbling ideas down and "winging it," especially if you're a pro, is a valid strategy for low-attendance or low-risk situations such as an impromptu meeting in the hallway with coworkers or simple "updates" where the only requirement is relaying information. If you don't need to get approval or persuade someone, winging it should be just fine.

If you're doing a budget presentation for upper management, a keynote speech at a conference, or a startup business pitch for investors, there's just too much to lose.

So let's get a five-step format to fit all of your awesome ideas in and a training regimen to rehearse with to save the day and make you a hero!

How to Create Content for the Speech

In 2013, As Seen On TV products like the Snuggie, the ShamWow, P90X, and others earned more than $5 billion, and many of us are their happy customers.[4]

If the promotion is so aesthetically cheesy, with a repetitive formulaic structure and products that (allegedly) don't endure the test of time, why does the concept work? And what can we learn from them?

Simple.

They use a time-tested model of persuasion called *Monroe's motivated sequence*[5] that *you* can use to make effective pitches for startups, products, or any idea at any meeting you'll ever attend.

---

[4] Lia Sestric, "The Most Profitable 'As Seen on TV' Products of All Time," Yahoo! Finance, August 26, 2019, https://finance.yahoo.com/news/most-profitable-seen-tv-products-090000530.html.

[5] Alan H. Monroe, *Principles and Types of Speech*, 5th ed. (Chicago: Scott Foresman, 1962).

MONROE'S MOTIVATED SEQUENCE

ATTENTION

First of all, get my attention
on the
Problem immediately. Make
me care, make me focused on
this one thing alone.

NEED

Elaborate the problem by
telling me why
it can't wait.
And why it is harmful to
myself and others
I care for.

SATISFACTION

Now I am aware of the
problem, and want to
fix it, what can I do
about it?

VISUALIZATION

Describe this solution in the most
vivid terms. Calm all doubts
regarding implementation and
make me "see" the results in
action.

ACTION

Make a
proposal – give me a timeline,
numbers, charts, projections.
Reward me for quick and
decisive action, get me to
take concrete steps.

Figure 2. Monroe's motivated sequence.
Use this format to put your speech together.

This structure of speaking is perfect for anyone who is trying to change their audience's mind (i.e., make a persuasive speech).

Any idea you communicate on policy requires someone's agreement, which is like making a sale. To get the sale, achieve consensus using your persuasive marketing: attain their attention, solve their problem, and use push-pull mechanisms to induce action. And all in *five easy steps.*[6]

1. *Get their attention.*

First of all, get my attention on the problem *immediately.*

Your audience is distracted with many competing thoughts, so the first challenge is to break distraction and create focus on one idea, which is this looming problem that can't be ignored.

The most effective way infomercials do this is by giving a *strong, strident visual*—a mess that needs cleaning, distressed people, lack of happiness, and so on.

Points of Focus

- What is wrong?
- What are you trying to fix?

2. *Establish the need.*

People hate change. So you have to argue for it.

Even if you focus on the problem, getting movement on it is hard because our habits and behaviors are so entrenched that we will make adjustments to lessen the problem but not major changes to eliminate it completely.

So elaborate the problem by telling me why it can't wait and why it is harmful to myself and others I care for.

---

[6] Combine this logic format with the general speaking format described in chapter 1.

Points of Focus

- What consequences lie ahead if I don't change?
- What harm is being caused at the moment?
- Who is at risk?

3. *Satisfy the need.*

Now that I am aware of the problem and *want* to fix it, what can I do about it?

With any problem, there can be competing concerns or variables. Ergo, there are competing solutions. In a finance meeting, you may have some people vying for cost-cutting (except their own team's budget, of course) while others might say growing revenue is a better way to move forward.

As the speaker, it is up to you to quell the disagreements in people's minds. The best way to do that is to give people a complete plan to react to, with roles for individuals, timelines of work targets, and lists of deliverables to be achieved, as well as ways to measure success.

For some, agreement is easier than debate.

Points of Focus

- Why is your solution the *best* answer?
- How can I easily implement it?
- Is it fail-safe?

4. *Visualize the future.*

Describe this solution in the most vivid terms. Be sure to show, not just tell. Infomercials do this by showing the various uses of their product, comparing options, competitors, prices, illustrating how your lifestyle will improve. Your idea shouldn't just fix a problem; it should underscore some mission in keeping with the culture of the organization.

More importantly, your audience should see this *clearly and memorably.*

Points of Focus

- Show the success of the idea
- Calm doubts regarding implementation
- Underscore effectiveness and appropriateness

5. *Close the deal!*

OK, you have my tacit agreement. Now force my hand to vote for your plan.

Make a proposal in concrete terms: give me a timeline, numbers, charts, projections—anything that will make me devote my time and/ or money. Infomercials show how quick action (*buy now!*) can improve results, and they give incentives like free gifts as well. Reward me for quick and decisive action, and make the plan time sensitive. That's the only way to get someone to sign on the dotted line!

Points of Focus

- Convince me that acting now is the only way I can benefit fully from this plan.
- Tell me how your competitors cannot match you for value or even come close!
- Earn the trust of your audience by offering a discount or some personal gesture of good faith. Make me feel special!

✍ Getting Ready for the Presentation

This can't be accomplished without preparation. For this practice regimen, you will need a pen, paper, a recording device or app, a stopwatch or timer app, a quiet room, and a half- or full-size mirror.

1. *Script it (and keep it for later as well).*

Write the whole thing out one time. Yes, the *whole* thing. Don't worry, though. It's OK if you stray from the *exact* wording in small, grammatical ways when you say it out aloud on the big day, just so long as we do this step-by-step the first time.

Expert tip: To save time, use speech-to-text. Most smartphones, word processing software, and so on, have this function. You can spell-check later.

Use your own vocabulary, what you're comfortable with. Oh, and you'll probably read it a couple of times, change a few phrases, and cut entire paragraphs or even entire pages. That's OK. Keep at it until you have it written out, with all the information you need to be in it, a solid intro, and a conclusion.

By now you have a fully written draft for your speech. (Feel free to rewrite it if needed at this point.)

Read it out aloud from the paper several times. This not only places it clear in your mind (we often have a photographic input, however slight) but also helps you create a mental order of things.

As you do, make note of the first word or key phrase in each paragraph and try to associate that word or phrase to the whole paragraph. Eventually, put each key phrase in sequence on a single piece of paper in a bulleted list format. Add any additional words you may need with any of the bullets to make them flow in your mind.

By now you have a fully written (or rewritten) draft for your speech and a single sheet of paper with the speech in bulleted list format.

2. *Do a "mic check."*

Use a sound or video recording device, perhaps a smartphone app (usually preinstalled), and record yourself reading the speech aloud. Use a pair of good headphones (sound-blocking if possible) to check your voice quality.

- *Voice recorder:* Listen to your disembodied voice to catch mistakes you *won't* catch in video. Keep a tally of filler words like "uh," "um," "like," and so on.
- *Video recorder:* Watch your eye contact. Are you looking at the audience consistently and across the whole room? Are your hands moving to illustrate your points and to regulate the momentum of delivery?

Ask yourself these key questions:

1. Am I loud enough?
2. Am I pronouncing each word correctly?
3. Is my tone pleasant and appropriate to the context?

To determine appropriateness of volume, have a friend or two listen to the audio playback. They should be able to hear every word without straining.

When you listen to the audio, stop whenever you hear an error and reread that sentence aloud into a separate recording file. Once you've read through the whole thing and practiced each error out loud, we're ready to proceed.

By now you have a fully written draft for your speech, a single sheet of paper with the speech in bulleted list format, and an audio and/or video recording of your speech.

3. *Take the memory challenge, one step at a time.*

Think about the best speeches you've ever heard. What are some of the qualities that made them great?

Certainly it was things like word choice, vocal tone, the topic itself, the setting, and most of all, the speaker sounding unrehearsed. Speaking from the heart. Just like they were having a personal conversation with you. *Natural.*

This style, called *extemporaneous speaking*, includes situations in which you knew in advance of the speaking opportunity and might even have some notes or materials prepared to help you deliver the speech.

Don't get me wrong. Writing out a speech like we talked about earlier is essential for big occasions and for beginning speakers in general.

Yet you deliberately do *not* memorize the speech or talk in order to sound normal, read the room, and form your words accordingly.

Take it one paragraph at a time. Try to say it aloud without looking down. Then add another and then another. See how many you can say without forgetting. It will take a while, sure, but you'll really get it!

Expert tip: You might find yourself ad-libbing a little here and there.

That's OK. Keep recording to be sure you're only ad-libbing for fluidity and not losing content or context.

4. *Get your stopwatch ready, and take the time challenge.*

By now you have your speech written, vetted for errors, checked for pronunciation, and even partly memorized. (It's OK at this point if you have one or two problem spots. Those will only go away with repeated practice.) Most speeches have a time limit, and if they don't, you should make an estimate and set one.

To ensure you stay within your allotted time, a good approach is to break your speech into three segments:

1. Introduction—One-fifth of a typical speech
2. Body—Three-fifths of a typical speech
3. Conclusion—One-fifth of a typical speech

So a five minute speech would have one minute of intro, three minutes of body, and a one-minute conclusion.

Apply this formula to the length of your speech and then adjust as needed. For example, longer lectures that go for an hour might have a longer body section.

Depending on your information and its complexity; the degree of awareness, interest, or expertise your audience has on the topic; and the occasion itself, I'd say ten minutes is a safe speech length for most occasions, less if possible. More than ten minutes is fine if the amount of information is too great and requires further explanation.

We're now in the final lap. This step may seem like a repeat of step 4 (memory), but we're not just trying to get through more and more of the speech without error. We're also watching for time.

Expert tip: always ask yourself how you can reduce word count in your speeches or make them shorter.

Have someone time you (so you are not distracted from your speech) or use a stopwatch to time yourself. Let's say the first run goes for ten minutes. Now ask yourself to do the same speech in eight minutes. Then push yourself to seven minutes! Then six minutes!

At some point after three or more rehearsals, your brain, which has been shaving off extra bits here and there to keep up with the pressure, will run out of things to leave out without cutting entire subtopics. *That's the ideal time for this speech.*

Another tip: If even after this exercise you still find yourself going over the allotted time, just leave out a few subtopics and introduce them in the Q&A session or via a pre- or postspeech email to the attendees or via slides. Basically by any other medium outside the main speech.

5. *Look in the mirror to practice your expressions.*

Your face is paramount for a speech. Each expression conveys an emotion, adds to the tone of the context, and includes the audience (through eye contact) and makes them *part* of the speech.

So now we repeat step 5 (time challenge) but while looking into a mirror. (You should at least be able to see your torso.) Practice your smile; you're happy to be here! Move your hands around just a bit to help illustrate your ideas; be careful to use open palms—not extended fingers or fists—moved in slow, gentle motions. Add gestures thoughtfully at the right points in your speech where movement of your hands adds emphasis to the idea.

Practice your entire speech now, recording (via video if possible) and timing it, remembering the expressions and gestures as well.

Here's a key point: do *not* practice less than three times or more than seven times. In my experience, if you practice less than three times, your brain won't be able to map out the ideas in order and you won't be able to speak fluently without your notes. If you practice more than seven times, your brain will tire of the speech and you'll lose the passion in your voice, sound less natural, and lose the interest of the audience.

Expert tip: Even if you only have a short time beforehand, warm up for your speech (it can also help you deal with any anxiety). Walk up and down a hallway or up and down a flight of stairs. If walking is not an option, do some deep breathing. Breathe deeply, hold your breath for one second, exhale, and repeat at least three times. Be sure to stretch your arms, legs, and neck—whatever is possible. And drink a glass of water!

By now, the key goal is to know your speech well enough to

remember the sequence of ideas but not so much that you lose the zing that comes from you enjoying something you're still passionate about.

Final Thoughts

The best way to do well in a speech under pressure is to focus on how much you care about the ideas you're talking about, and to use the simplest language to make the biggest point.

Simple and passionate wins *every time*.

3
STORYTELLING

 What Is a Story?

A story is an *experience* that we know of, or that happened to us, which we are relating to another person or persons to make them *feel as if they were there.*

The emotional connection to the situation and characters, the peril of the conflict, and finally, the relief when the conflict is resolved—this set of feelings is what makes for a great story.

The roller-coaster journey teaches us about our own humanity and shows growth, change, and evolution in how we see ourselves and what we do.

Most of all, we *all* learn something.

Purpose of Storytelling in the Workplace

It's pretty simple. If you want people to be interested in what you have to say, if you want them to buy into something, change their minds, or just even care about it, you have to get their interest.

So just like your favorite blockbuster movie, a story at work has to be about people or teams facing, say, a difficult project, their response (actions that hopefully resolve the problem), and the result, which offers closure in terms of success or failure, lessons learned, and next steps to keep improving and growing.

Here are a few examples of work situations that need a story:

☐ A report on a project your team just concluded
☐ A pitch to executives to green light a project
☐ An ask for increased budget, higher head count, or some other kind of permission
☐ Change management of any kind
☐ Making the case for your or someone else's hiring or promotion
☐ Job interviews

A great story must have these core elements:

1. Structure and content
2. Pacing and details
3. An ending

Let's start our journey to tell a great work story!

✏️ Determining Structure and Content

A method that has been a great winner, in my experience, is the STAR method. This method, per studies, seems to bring out the full value of one's experience and significantly increases performance, and is a better predictor of performance than pure intelligence.[7]

STAR stands for *situation, task, action, and result.*

---

[7] Ed Pulakos and Neall Schmitt, "Experience-Based and Situational Interview Questions: Studies of Validity," *Personnel Psychology* 48 (May 1995): 289–308, https://onlinelibrary.wiley.com/doi/abs/10.1111/j.1744-6570.1995.tb01758.x.

STAR METHOD

1. SITUATION

We start describing the
background, setting
the stage.

2. TASK

Talk specifically about
the challenge we're
facing.

3. ACTION

What are we doing to
move ahead with the
goals of the Task?
Mention at least 3
concrete goals .

4. RESULT

What's happening in the end?
What were the measurable
outcomes?
Tell us next
steps and wrap it up .

Figure 3. STAR method for storytelling

The overall idea is to walk the audience through a set of circumstances that posed a challenge, describing the problem or project in detail, perhaps the threat it posed to your team's or company's success, and then detailing the proposed or completed response to the threat.

The key is to show not just your success in ending the conflict, but also to highlight your specific problem-solving abilities, such as working under pressure, working with minimum resources and/or supervision, and most of all, your communication skills.

Now you get it: The story isn't just saying, "We did it." Rather, it's saying, "Here's how we did it," and "These are some skills I demonstrated that saved the day."

We start with the *situation*, describing the background, setting the stage: "Our data analysis would take too long, customers would be irate and file complaints, and we would have a backlog of data requests."

Then we move to the *task*, where we talk specifically about the challenge we're facing: "So we tried to figure out how to decrease the backlog, increase the data testing speed, and increase customer satisfaction."

Next is *action*, what are we doing to move ahead with the goals of the task? Mention at least three concrete goals you have in mind, along with the plan you have to achieve them: "We put out an emergency request to our testing vendors for upgrades and solutions, got the budget request approved for the new data solution, and borrowed one team member on loan from another division to help us over the weekend while we ported over the data."

Finally, we have *results*. What's happening here in the end? What were the measurable outcomes? Give me a set of results, who did or said what, what the next steps are, and wrap it up with a neat bow by summarizing the whole thing in one line. Remember to mix narrative or subjective results with numerical or objective results, about half and half. For example, "We now have an easier method to analyze marketing data, and our speed of running tests went up 34 percent."

COMMUNICATION MEANS TALKING TOGETHER

✍ How This Works

Situation and *task* serve as the *introduction*, ending with the task, similar to the thesis statement of any essay: a single line that summarizes what needs to be done and foreshadows the outcome of the story itself.

The main *actions* taken, along with the reasoning behind choosing those actions, as well as the trial-and-error process of figuring out the solutions to the problem, are the main *body* of the story.

Try to break this body up into three pieces. That seems to give us enough to talk about without monotony and shows a variety of remedies taken, demonstrating the thoroughness of your analysis in understanding the problem, as well as in planning and executing the solution.

Results (along with next steps) give us a *conclusion*, a way to recap the entire story by reminding us what the main problem(s) consisted of, what actions were taken, and what measurable outcomes were achieved.

✍ Managing Pacing

Pacing in a story is key, and there's fortunately a few small things you can do to make it work for your audience.

1. *Transitions*

Between each segment, such as the three actions you elected to take in the body of the story, there should be a line that connects the final thought of the prior portion and gives us a reason and direction to move further into your story.

This could go something like "... once we had completed the debugging of the program, we had to start working on the safe reupload of the files to the main server ..." Think of this like being on the highway and seeing a sign that says, "Now leaving New York," and then eventually seeing a sign that says, "Welcome to Connecticut."

The key: So we smoothly jump from section to section, and as an added bonus, you give "reminders" to your audience (i.e., this is what we *just* finished talking about, and this is what we'll talk about *next*."

2.   *Time Balance*

We talked about this briefly in a prior chapter, and it's worth a recap. You essentially divide the story up into equal sections and spend enough time on each section (one to two minutes average) and, when in doubt, keep the whole speech about five to ten minutes long.

Extra tip: When presenting to senior leadership, *always* have the two-minute version of your story ready to go. Essentially just give the top-line summary using the STAR method—situation, task, action, result—with next steps. And you're done!

3.   *Visual and Proof-Based Details*

Details normally slow things down. So why mention them in pacing? Well, actually, *visual details* are essential inclusions for correct pacing. That includes talking about color, shape, size, technique, and so on. *Proof-based details* explain the why and the how of your story, mixing just the right amount of subjective and objective data.

Too little detail and the story feels abrupt and raises too many questions because of lack of proof or confusion because people can't imagine the things you're talking about.

Too many details and we lose momentum and the story feels never-ending.

So you need the right amount and type of visual and proof-based details to help your audience imagine what you're describing and agree with your reasoning.

So how can you know what details are needed? And in what quantity?

Here are a few types of details to include:

- Details that help us visualize the problem in one line: "the delivery chain is weak with a backlog of old orders and causing delays in new orders."
- Details that help us visualize the solution in one line, talking through each action step: "We need to fire fight for now while

we overhaul the supply chain. Let's start by making irate customers happy again with shipping costs credited back to them ..."

- Details that help us visualize the results, including some hard numbers, some qualitative improvements, and next steps: "If we follow this plan, we will expand order capacity by 14 percent and simplify the customer experience, and we just need your approval for the budget."

✎ Nailing the Ending

Spoiler alert! The ending of any story is the *best* part. It's the surprise, the satisfying conclusion of a long and arduous journey, the solving of a mystery, the defeat of a challenge.

So how do we end a work story? Keep it simple:

- ☐ Remind us what has been accomplished with measurable results.
- ☐ Relay the roles played by each person.
- ☐ State the lessons that have been learned.
- ☐ List future steps being planned.
- ☐ Give us a *vision* of things to come with an optimistic tone that is unifying and inspiring.

For example, "We are elated that this project was completed on time and under budget, saving 13.5 percent in productivity costs as well as decreasing our error rate by 2 percent. The team really came together and put in the time, and now we can look ahead to expanding the new protocol out to other business units for a company-wide lift in efficiency."

Think about it: Stories are mostly about the passage of time. There is a distant past, a recent past (or present), and a future. Or, more precisely, a beginning, middle, and end.

So then the beginning or introduction of a story—the situation and task—becomes the past, setting the stage. The middle journey of the story—the action—becomes the present (even if recently concluded).

And the ending, though it also may have concluded, talks about and represents the future.

✍ Closing Thoughts

One other kind of detail worth mentioning is emotional detail. You may wonder how you can include emotion in a work-based story?

Try something like this: "Everything else was working fine late on Friday, but the data analytic dashboard was a mess. Jess jumped on it and cleaned it up over the weekend and made sure we were ready to go on Monday. The project stayed on track. Thanks, Jess. You're awesome!"

Just try it. Mention your team members' names and thank them for their effort and hard work. Maybe mention something specific that they did to help get the win.

Stories are about people's lives and about the events that shape those lives. Thus, it is about meaningfulness. If you can make your team and the work you do meaningful, your team will be transformed into a unit, you will have advertised the powerful culture of your team, and you will have become a leader.

4

SPEAKING OFF THE CUFF

Sometimes a speaking opportunity can sneak up on us, especially when we are interacting with a very senior executive.

A lot of people freeze up in such situations and end up using a lot of filler words—uh, um, like—rambling, and not really making a point.

And the other person stops listening after about thirty seconds.

This kind of moment is literally what the term *elevator pitch* was coined for—a sudden, unexpected chance to show your great idea, get it approved, and prove your worth.

These days we use the term *elevator pitch* to refer to all business meeting situations (so not literally in an elevator) in which you have a brief amount of time to talk to an important person and you have to structure your ideas simply and influentially to gain their approval.

If you combine it all, one of the most sought-after communication abilities is coming up with an on-the-spot response that impresses the listener, especially if they're an important person.

We use a lot of slang terms to describe this—winging it, speaking off the cuff, improvising—but it is known as *impromptu speaking*.

Impromptu speaking is the style you adopt in the situation where you didn't expect to be speaking or you didn't really know what you would be speaking about (e.g., being called on in class or in a meeting, receiving an unexpected phone call, or participating in a job interview).

Here you rely not on prepared notes but rather on your well-established knowledge of a given topic, maybe one that you're an expert on, and an overall manner that establishes your credibility, confidence, and command of the situation.

More importantly, you'll succeed with this style if you're the type of person who knows their own thoughts and opinions on a variety of relevant topics so that with little notice you can express yourself in a couple of minutes, doing so clearly and with impact.

✍ How Can I Be a Good Impromptu Speaker?

IMPROMPTU SPEAKING

1. Open with a Clear Decision
summarizing big picture

2. Use Short
Sentences

3. Clear format
(use star
method)

4. Tell a story or make a list
(or both)

5. Be Natural

6. Be Aware

Figure 4. Tips to speak off the cuff

First and foremost, realize that preparedness for speaking situations is the key. Even if you don't know a speaking situation is coming up, your knowledge of the subject matter and your ability to express it concisely in the spur of the moment are key to your success.

The secret to acing the impromptu speech is being clear and interesting, and ending quickly (usually two minutes is good). A few simple tips can help us form our ideas, prepare our story in our minds, and simplify the delivery for maximum impact.

1. *Identify a clear decision and opinion statement that summarizes the overall big picture.*

If you can't summarize the whole discussion in a single line, then your idea isn't ready and it's just a jumbled mess.

This single line in the beginning of your talk frames the whole discussion. It tells me what I most likely need to know, and the remainder of the speech is the details, proof, evidence, and next steps.

What's more, if I agree with this opening statement of yours, I might not even need to hear anything more, and this saves us all some time!

Try one of these templated thesis or summary statements (your topic is probably going to fit one):

- "We did X because Y and we got Z result(s)."
- "We successfully completed X with Y percent profit, and next we will do Z."
- "We need permission to do X because it has Y benefits and our proposed budget is Z with the following spending plan."

The key: In these impromptu situations, you have to remember that people are tremendously impatient and might even be stressing out about the results. If we give them the important information right up top, it cuts all the tension and puts everyone at ease. To do this well, always try to find out what's most important to your team members and leaders; that way you'll always know what to tell them first!

2. *Use short sentences.*

The most ineffective approach you can take is the long rambling run-on sentence: "So we did this, then we did this, and ... and ..."

There's a number of things wrong with this.

First, it doesn't give you a chance to breathe, so you'll sound monotonous.

Short sentences with one-second pauses in the middle will allow you to breathe, let the audience ask questions if relevant, and give audience members' brains a chance to process what they've just heard before you move on to the next topic. And, because you took a breath between your short sentences, you are able to pause and reduce the number of times you say a filler word, stay on track (and not ramble), and avoid repeating yourself.

The key: Use the opening statement as the summary and one to two short sentences as the reasons why the summary statement is true. For instance, "Our projections tell us that the next financial quarter will be 10 percent above target. This is due to increased consumer spending, cost-cutting in engineering, and a successful online marketing campaign."

This allows the listener to feel more convinced that you are correct, and it also allows you to create the flow of the speech more easily in your mind.

3. *Follow a clear format.*

Our brains, when put on the spot, often don't know when to begin. Imagine yourself driving on the road and then suddenly all the street signs are gone. There's just the road. Or worse, no road, just open land. Where does one go next? This is what leads to panic.

Don't reinvent the wheel!

Now, just as the roads and signs give us a direction in which to steer our cars, the templates we've talked about in this book's earlier chapters give us a chance to know what should come first, next, and last in any short speech.

Let's review.

We've talked about how you can use the STAR (situation, task, action, result)[8] method for storytelling. Tell us the background, the challenge, the action taken to solve the problem, and the outcomes (with next steps). Done!

Talking about organizational change? You can use the model in the decision, pro-con, sell, and tell method[9] (or speak of it in the past tense). Or you can use a version of the Monroe's motivated sequence (attention, need, satisfaction, visualization, and action) [10]method to persuade the audience and spur them into action.

The key: Whatever your speech goal may be, select the template that works best for you and insert content into each section. This will save valuable time and brain energy, which you can then put toward the wording of your message.

4. *Use stories and lists.*

OK, so now you have a format and some kind of starting point. What content can we use?

There's basically two kinds of content: stories and lists.

Stories are used to make a point and establish credibility, while lists summarize facts and information. Stories explain who and why, and lists give us the what, when, and how.

Use your imagination to remember the *main* concern about a project and build your story around it. Who was involved? How did they react?

When describing your solution to the problem and/or next steps, that's where you can use a list. You can order the list in terms of time (chronologically).

The key: Combine the two for best results. For instance, "The team was dangerously close to missing the deadline when we switched our method from A to B. That allowed us to dissect the data faster, and it gave us three results, X, Y and Z. We are moving on to further testing to confirm."

---

[8] See chapter 3.
[9] See chapter 8.
[10] See chapter 2.

5. *Focus on flow.*

The most important thing to remember is that this speech or presentation has to feel *natural*. We do that by structuring and pacing the whole activity, keeping it short, keeping it engaging and interactive, and "handing off the baton" to your listener(s) or to the next person to speak. To ensure smooth flow, keep the following three elements in mind:

a. *Overall manner:* Communicate agreement and cooperation, and that you're in control of the situation and grateful for the help you get. You can do this by using words and phrases like *simply, on time, successfully, meet expectations,* or more slang versions like *we've got this.* Some kinds of phrases are multipurpose. My personal favorites include *no worries* and *we'll get it done",* which convey anticipated success, control, and also a kind of team feeling.

b. *Timing:* Break it into an introduction, three main ideas, and a conclusion, all about equal length, just like any other speech. Not sure how long to speak? Shorter is best. If the expectations are not clear, keep it to about two minutes and certainly less than five. You can always go into detail when asked specific questions.

c. *The ending:* Give people a recap at the end, and your final statement should have a positive, future-oriented tone. Lastly, ask the listener a question (even one as simple as "What are your thoughts?") to get their input next and keep the conversation going.

6. *Maintain your expertise level.*

How can you be ready for something you don't know is coming? By maintaining awareness at every level:

a. *Product and industry awareness (for team leaders):* Read up on the latest innovations and information about your industry. Subscribe to websites, newsletters, and periodicals. You should know your company's products and services and how they rank up against competitors. What are the competitive gaps? How can we get more customers and keep them?

b. *Company and team awareness:* Do you know which teams and team leaders are responsible for what functions? What are some distinctions between similar teams? Who would you approach to solve which of your problems? It's amazing how different, strange bits of information can give us a way forward. Tribal knowledge is the concept that groups have elders (experienced team members) who keep knowledge and can pass it on. If we are aware of and acquainted with those elders, this knowledge can really help us in a tight spot.

c. *Self-awareness:* How well do you know yourself? Your strengths and weaknesses? Your accomplishments?

As an exercise, try to write down and summarize your personal introduction. If you met someone at a networking event or business meeting and they didn't know you or what you did, how would you describe yourself? Think of your name, your title, what your job involves, your recent or biggest accomplishments, the size of team you manage (if applicable), what you're working on (show your capabilities!), and your vision for your team's future.

For example, "Hello, I'm Megan. I'm the senior engineer for IT at Bizco Inc. We're a payments processor for e-commerce platforms, and I manage the security protocols for mobile transactions. I've got a team of eight engineers, and we're getting ready for integrating blockchain into our processes."

This small script you can make for your personal introduction will help you break the ice with anyone you meet in the elevator or anywhere else.

This technique of scripting will also help you prepare little quick ready-to-go answers to present a listener with at any time.

Remember, the best way to speak off the cuff is to *always* be prepared to speak.

✐ In Closing

I get it. Sometimes you don't have all the answers.

Let's say a situation comes up and you don't know how to respond. No problem!

Don't fake an answer.

Instead, show your worth by responding with a smart question: "How do we accomplish this while being in compliance with X law?" Or by framing it as the problem you're working on. This way, at least if you don't have the answer, your leadership knows that you're diagnosing the problem correctly, which *any good leader* will tell you is half the battle.

Next, ask the leader for their input. Who knows? The leader might want to mentor you!

It's OK if you don't have the answers. We all have to research to figure answers out bit by bit. All you can do is persevere and give it your best shot.

There's *no easy way*.

But it is worth it.

PART 2

LEADERSHIP

5

DEFINING LEADERSHIP

Every person who is good at their job and works hard gets an opportunity to be a leader at some point. But for some people, this is their worst nightmare.

Being "in charge" of a project—or, to make matters worse, in charge of *other people*—is terrifying.

"What if I make a bad decision? Everyone will blame, dislike, and disrespect me."

At the heart of it, whether you're the owner of a small corner store with two employees or the leader of a country, fear of failure and judgment is the biggest challenge to overcome.

Having worked with corporate leaders of all types, I can tell you a secret: *All leaders, even good ones, make mistakes from time to time.*

It's not about getting them all right; it's about learning to decrease the error percentage, finding consistent approaches that streamline the process, and knowing which decisions make more impact so that they get more time and resources.

Let's learn what leadership truly means, identify what gaps exist in our leadership techniques and methods, find our leadership style, and then optimize that style for success.

✐ What Is Leadership?

Sometimes the best way to define something is to define what it isn't. Leadership is *not* the same as managing.

LEADERS > MANAGERS

MANAGERS   LEADERS

Managers have tasks

Leaders have Vision

Managers control for mistakes

Leaders unlock potential

Managers focus on the bottom line

Leaders create value

(c) Culture of Speak
CultureofSpeak.com

Figure 5. Differences between leaders and managers

Managing requires a mindset of control and organization. It requires knowing the task(s) at hand, preventing or reducing negatives like errors and costs, and maximizing positives like profits and sale or production rates.

To be sure, managing is very important and a hard job to do.

It's just that when it comes to really succeeding at work or in life, everyone needs a person to be *more* than a manager.

They need someone to take that profit, which is in terms of money, and make it into *value*, which is the fulfillment of needs, wants, and desires. The more value your employees get out of working for you, the more loyal they will be. The more your customers feel you care about them, the less likely they will be to buy from your competitors.

People need someone who can take a group of people who work together and transform them into a well-oiled machine that functions *as if it were a single person*.

In other words, a *team*.

Managers can brainstorm ideas; leaders have a fully formed concept for future success, called a *vision*.

Finally, managers give work to others, while leaders *unlock the potential* of their teams by mentoring, coaching, and making each team member believe in the commonly held vision for success.

✐ Defining Leadership

Leadership is a *quality* that people possess, and one that may or may not be given in the form of a title (e.g., CEO). It is a quality that involves having a vision and taking responsibility for delivering results. To do this, leaders create or propagate the *culture* of the organization and help unify all the people that work in the organization around commonly held ideas, beliefs, and most of all, the unifying vision.

It's really worth thinking about: the more people in a company share ways of thinking, ways of judging right and wrong, and ways to take right action, the more they act in unity toward the common goal and help achieve the vision.

This is why leadership is a daunting role to play and is not for everyone.

Yet if we take it on, it can be the most rewarding experience of our lives.

So what are some simple things we can do to be great leaders?

✍ Leadership Audit

The first step we can take toward being a great leader is recognizing our strengths and weaknesses, finding the gaps, and then working to remove them.

Top Challenges

A long time ago, when I was in college, I met a business consultant who taught me this great question: "What keeps you up at night?"

He used to ask it of his clients to try to narrow down their most pressing problems.

Even though it is framed as a specific question that may have a short answer, it cues the listener up to answer in the form of a laundry list.

So at this moment, take a paper and pen or pencil, and try to answer this question: *What keeps me up at night?*

In my experience, this leads to at least one main response, usually the first thing that comes to mind.

We find the one thing that is a recurring thorn in your side, something that has a *repetitive pattern and is like a chronic backache.* You have tried short-term fixes, but just like taking painkillers, the remedy itself can lead to a long-term problem.

One such problem may be delays in getting financial reports, which lead to delays in budget allocations, which lead to other strategic delays.

Let's make a note of this recurring problem and continue the process.

Ecosystem Analysis

The next step is a more thorough audit or analysis of your *ecosystem.* Ecosystem, here, refers to all the people we are connected to inside of our companies, some within our team or division, some above or below us, and some who are peers to us. Partly this is about our company's internal organizational structure, but it's also about the social relationships involved: Who is respected? Who isn't? Whom do you trust? Who's an expert on X product?

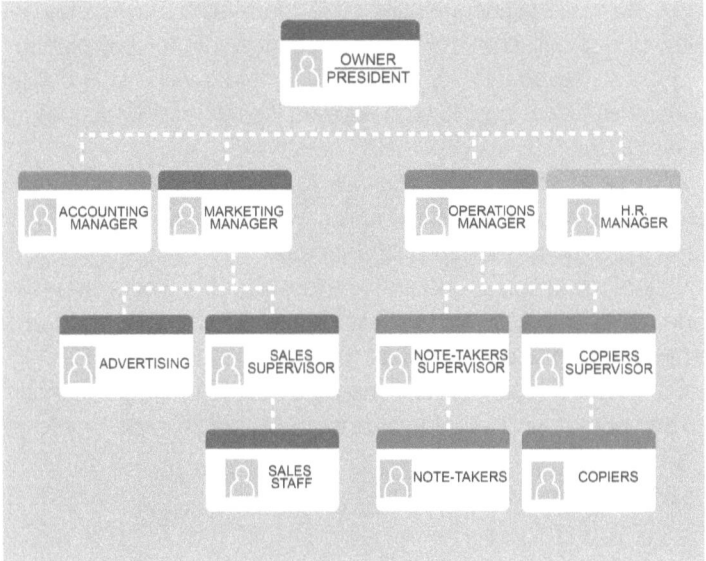

Figure 6. Example of an organizational chart

Just like in the animal kingdom, a corporate ecosystem is a web of relationships; each member needs each of the others to play their particular role in a symbiotic fashion. Everyone's contribution "stacks up," and collectively we deliver results.

For a typical corporate leader, your ecosystem might include your direct reports (people who answer to you), your supervisor, your peers, the next level of management, and some key people in related departments of the company. For some people, this may include suppliers and customers or other professionals with whom you work that are outside your organization.

Next, respond to these prompts:

1. Make a list of the top five people or entities with whom you most often interact.
2. What is *your* top need (or needs) from each one of them?
3. Which of *your* needs are they not meeting? Why or why not?
4. What is *their* top need (or needs) from you?
5. Which of *their* needs are you not meeting? Why or why not?

As you can imagine, gathering this information may involve a very healthy phone call, email, or in-person chat with each key person.

Each of the people you most often interact with—let's call them "stakeholders"—are people who have an interest in your success and vice versa.

With each stakeholder you talk to, even the fact that you are interested in improving relationships will give you a boost in that person's productivity and responsiveness.

One of my clients found that she just added a weekly ten-minute phone call with a key supplier, and three of her backlogged orders suddenly moved ahead and were fulfilled.

Contact is key to any relationship. Put time on your calendar for each key person and let them all know that they're important to you.

Time Management Analysis

Do you feel your time is efficiently and productively used?

Many of us are hardwired to think of time as something to be saved. And how we do this is by doing *more* things in *less* time.

The problem with this logic is that we sometimes forget that each of the things we do or accomplish has a different meaning and value.

Some things are more important; they must be done first. Others less so; they can wait. Some things might be pretty much optional; do them or not, it doesn't matter on the whole.

Think of your typical work week. On a sheet of paper or on your computer screen, chart out your work calendar.

Now try to categorize your calendar items by type. Some might be customer meetings, others are you meeting with your team to assign work, and a few more might be meeting with senior leadership. Finally, there is your own work.

Separately, make a list of the top projects or to-do list items that you're working on right now.

Next, answer these questions:

- Name your top three priority projects.
- What percentage of time do you give them? Estimates are fine. (Leave 20 percent aside for miscellaneous tasks.)

- Are your top three priorities getting at least 70 percent of your time?
- Is your number one priority getting at least 30–40 percent of your time?
- Can you narrow down that *one* relationship (person or team) that's an issue?

In my experience, you will likely find *one* project that is taking more time than you feel it is worth.

Identifying this item gives us something to think about, and we can think back to the last section of this chapter and reestablish the strong working relationship with the person in charge of that project.

Next, think about balance. The amount of time we give any project has to be a combination of the revenue or money that it generates (or losses it prevents) as well as the deadlines or risks that are associated with it.

Simply put, the more attention that senior leadership is giving it, or should be giving it, the more time that project deserves.

That said, each project or work item needs a *minimum* amount of your time per week or month, even if you have smartly delegated tasks to people who report to you. The rest is dependent on revenue and how time sensitive the project is.

Now, revisit your calendar.

What items do you wish to remove from it? Which ones would you add?

Some simple rules: give the maximum time to the work and people that are most valuable, yet ensure that you give a regular, minimum amount of time to each person or task, no matter how unimportant they may seem.

✎ A Leader's Tools for Success

Just like a machine, a leader has a few different "buttons" they can push or actions that they can take to motivate employees and create different outcomes.

The simplified version is that you can use a combination of rewards and punishments. Let's call them positive and negative incentives.

It's a basic psychological principle: when I do something you like and you reward me, I am motivated to repeat that "good" behavior and vice versa.

For this concept to work, it has to be fair and it needs minimum manual intervention from the supervisor, in that it becomes part of the culture itself. Everyone *knows* the rule and what it leads to, so everyone follows it because they want the positive incentives or rewards associated with it, or they want to avoid the punishments or negative incentives.

So what positive incentives might we use? The examples are easy to think of:

- Compensation (raises, bonuses, stocks, health benefits)
- Employee performance awards (employee of the month, top salesperson of the year, etc.)
- Promotions (including a change in title, which brings prestige)
- Agreeing to requests (e.g., additional days off or work from home flexibility)

The more you show your willingness to make such awards and the clearer and more transparent the rules are, the more motivated your workers will be to strive harder.

This list is mostly tangible benefits, things that are concrete. There are also intangible benefits, such as the sharing of knowledge or access credentials to some expensive software, being invited to an important meeting, or an introduction to an important person in the company.

Very frequently, the intangible benefits are actually better incentives because they don't require bureaucratic paperwork or other permissions and a leader can just do the needful in a single email or hallway conversation.

On the flip side, what negative incentives might we use? Typically the negative incentive is the denial or removal of a privilege. Consider the following:

- Attending an important meeting as a guest
- Access to information
- Hr-advised coaching

- Formal employee performance improvement plans (also called pips)
- Removal from the company

The only advice I would give here is to give the employee every chance to improve, document everything (to show you've followed through *and* to protect yourself from any accusations), and to know when time is up.

A simple rule might be to give no more than six months for the employee to turn around the undesirable behavior. In that time, plan three meetings that an HR representative attends along with you and the employee, and have the employee agree to an improvement plan.

If less than 70 percent of the items on the improvement plan (assuming they are of equal importance) are completed to satisfaction, then it is the end of the process and the employee should be let go.

Closing Thoughts

Much of our anxiety about leadership is that we lack a true mapping of the situation at hand and our role in it.

Leaders are best defined as people who get things done, who inspire others, and who hold up their assigned burdens consistently, effectively, and sometimes ingeniously.

The next step to leadership is knowing your team. We will learn how your team evolves over time and what role is needed from you at each stage.

By taking on the right role at the right time, you will always know how to communicate with the team, how much of an active role you need to take, and what the best way is to help your team reach its potential.

Next, let's talk about teams.

6
LEADING A TEAM

In the pre-dotcom era, prior to the 2000s, teams had strict vertical hierarchies and chains of command. Now, teams have flattened.[11] Often, team members are similar in rank and just have different specialties.

Some companies have tried systems in which the subject matter specialists most relevant to a project take charge, and so the "baton" changes hands when the type of project changes. Thus, leadership in this atmosphere is not connected to any one person but instead is a quality and a phenomenon. It's an ongoing aggregate of ideas, processes, and principles that through shared agreement—culture—is enacted by *all* members of the team.

As a result, the team is transported from being a simple grouping of people into a combination of abilities, talents, steps, and stages—in a sense, a cycle and process.

This is why it's essential to study teams along the lines of Tuckman's model[12]—with a key modification. Tuckman's model is a

---

[11] Dylan Walsh, "Rethinking Hierarchy in the Workplace," *Insights by Stanford Business,* September 25, 2017, https://www.gsb.stanford.edu/insights/rethinking-hierarchy-workplace.

[12] Bruce W. Tuckman, "Developmental Sequence in Small Groups," *Psychological Bulletin* 63, no. 6 (June 1965): 384–99, https://doi.org/10.1037/h0022100.

way of understanding how teams start, how they improve, and how they are adjourned or complete their role, so we can learn leadership attuned to the type of team and the stage of team, rather than any cookie-cutter model of leadership.

✍ Applying Tuckman's Model to Your Team

As a leader, manager, or even just someone in charge of a single meeting, it is your job to know the following:

1. What stage is your team at?
2. How far are they in their maturation process?
3. How does this particular meeting need to be successful ...
4. ... so that each team member performs at their highest capacity?

Leaders need to *know team members exceptionally well*, observing their connection to the team as a unitary whole.

We will take this a step further. Not only will we identify the team development stages based on the Tuckman model[13], but along the way we'll identify the communication style and leadership style that best fits that particular stage. Let's start!

Stage—Actions

1. Forming—Set important precedents.
2. Norming—Follow precedents and use them to drive compliance.
3. Storming—Experiencing conflict? Help team members reidentify group purpose.

---

[13] *Important:* You may notice that I have modified the model from Tuckman's original concept, which was "forming, storming, norming, performing." In the version we're working with, norming comes in second, followed by storming, performing, and adjourning. The reason for this modification is, given the fact that almost half a century has passed since Tuckman's publication, managers and leaders alike have become somewhat practiced in the process, *yet* something goes wrong, there is conflict and "storming," where a team is truly tested before it starts to work in full cooperation. You will see the reasons for this modification as we go more in depth.

4. Performing—Enforce action in progress, strong agenda, delegation, and roles.
5. Adjourning—Make acknowledgements, mark progress, continue relationships beyond.

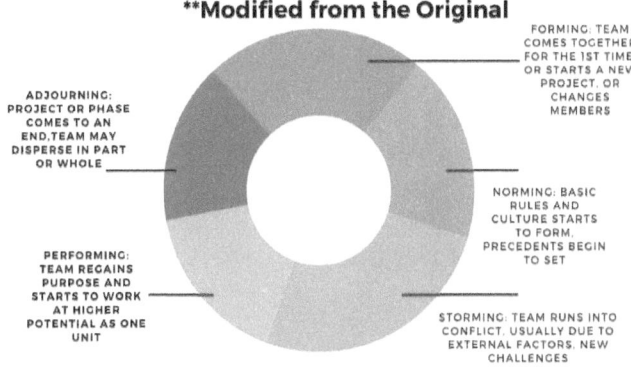

Tuckman's Team Development Model
**Modified from the Original

FORMING: TEAM COMES TOGETHER FOR THE 1ST TIME, OR STARTS A NEW PROJECT. OR CHANGES MEMBERS

ADJOURNING: PROJECT OR PHASE COMES TO AN END, TEAM MAY DISPERSE IN PART OR WHOLE

NORMING: BASIC RULES AND CULTURE STARTS TO FORM, PRECEDENTS BEGIN TO SET

PERFORMING: TEAM REGAINS PURPOSE AND STARTS TO WORK AT HIGHER POTENTIAL AS ONE UNIT

STORMING: TEAM RUNS INTO CONFLICT. USUALLY DUE TO EXTERNAL FACTORS, NEW CHALLENGES

Figure 7. Modified version of Tuckman's model of team development

1. *Forming—Set important precedents.*

Forming sounds simple enough: You're talking about the team coming together for the first time at work. They're going to feel a little bit of communication anxiety. Think of this as like having stage fright. And that's normal!

Sure, some of them may know each other socially. Perhaps they've done different projects together or worked on a similar project in the previous year. But there's going to be some amount of "new" to this team including but not limited to any of the following:

- New personnel
- New project
- New circumstances

- Emergency
- A different stage in an old project

Either way, when you have some "new," you're looking at some level of *uncertainty.*

So it is your job to make sure that the team is ready for it and it doesn't hold them back.

If your team is at the forming stage, the most important thing to focus on is the creation of new precedents.

How to do this right:

- Take company and legal policies and distill them down to easy-to-follow maxims.
- Understand learning and communication styles.
- Set purpose of the group and go over timeline of entire project or team cycle.

2.   *Norming—Follow precedents and use them to drive compliance.*

Norming is the process of normalizing precedents. It is the many small gestures or comments, reminders, emails, memos, and company events that all together build (or try to build) a cohesive company culture of rules and behaviors.

At the beginning of the team, the uncertainty, cold feet, and lack of knowledge makes it difficult to go forward. Now, people are aware of the policies but not very effective in enforcing them.

For leaders, norming is a particular challenge because of the modern expectation that "companies are like families." In addition, most workplaces tend to face some amount of unexpected challenges from the economy, social conditions, and the company's competitive environment.

The worst damage to norming is when the leader him- or herself does not follow written rules. If you are not following the rules that you are setting, they will not be followed, period.

If you do not correct people who knowingly or unknowingly, innocently or maliciously break the rules, then norms fail.

Remember: This is like creating relationships both for tasks and relationships. You have to get to know each other socially as much as coworkers. You know I like sushi, sure, but you should also know that I am a "big-picture thinker." Both are equally important!

How to do this right:

- Anticipate all reasonable situations. Plan rules.
- Create easy-to-access resources, much like having fire extinguishers clearly marked and visible.
- Monitor your personality types and set team roles accordingly.
- Make subteams as necessary to distribute the work. (Every meeting can't be all-hands.)
- Model good behavior yourself.
- Reward good norming.

3. *Storming—Experiencing conflict? Help team members reidentify the group purpose.*

Storming, as you can possibly imagine, has to do with the point in the team's life cycle where they've gotten over the ice-breaking portion and have created and enforced and are starting to follow some rules, but now the real chaos, the real test, the real challenge, begins.

Often this is when some team members are not following the rules or are not hitting their metrics. Or perhaps there is so much change happening so quickly in the team that precedents created in the norming process are simply not being followed. A typical example of this might be requiring that employees "clock in" and "clock out," say, at 9:00 a.m. and 5:00 p.m., but people amble in ten minutes late or leave ten minutes early, and then slowly, because of a poor system of checking, the infractions pile up and no one faces questions or penalties. So even if an important meeting is called at 9:15 a.m., one might not be sure to have the whole team present. And then there are the typical "but X said it was OK!" retorts when someone is questioned.

Perhaps things are so uncertain that there is simply no frame of reference to do effective problem-solving. This is when you, the leader with the vision, the effectiveness, the primacy of authority, can step in.

How to do this right:

- Make sure everyone remembers and recreates the original purpose of this team.
  - o   Why was it formed?
  - o   Why were these individuals chosen?
  - o   What were the norms they agreed to?
  - o   Why did they agree to those norms?

And this is where we really understand something key: the team isn't a grouping; it's an entirely separate entity from each of the people involved in it and the person leading it or even those dependent upon it.

When you join a team, you make a compact with this extrapersonal entity, this grouping of shared beliefs, ideals, and goals. That compact is forgotten in the rough-and-tumble of deadlines and personal ambitions.

This is where the leader has to make all the team members look outside of themselves, above themselves, and around themselves:

1.   What have we achieved?
2.   What have we done to disappoint ourselves?
3.   How have we fallen behind?

Regaining the sense of purpose as a team is very hard to do, and it takes a special leader to pull it off, sometimes.

How to do this right:

- Break away from the "eye of the storm." Leave the conference room for fresh air together.
- Talk abstractly if discussion was concrete; talk concretely if the discussion was abstract.
- Reframe the entire meaning of the discussion in a group and long-term sense.

This sense of purpose, the sense of history, the sense of collective agreement and collective impact upon each other and on the team as a whole can really turn around any kind of stressful team situation.

4. *Performing—Enforce action in progress, strong agenda, delegation, and roles.*

Now we come to the penultimate stage: performing. On the surface it might sound like your team is, shall we say, doing its job. Sounds simple, right? Well, the reason the team is doing its job is because you have successfully traversed all three previous stages.

The major conflict or chaos that could have happened has been weathered. The first thing you must do is ensure that you continue the good work, as it only takes a single error to lose a good deal of progress.

How to do this right:

- *Clear tasks*—Know exactly what work needs to be done.
- *Clear roles*—Clearly delegate and the enforce people's roles
- *Continued positive norming*—Remind the team what they are doing correctly and remind them consciously to repeat good behaviors.
- *Team responsibility*—Emphasize that each team member is ultimately responsible to the team as a whole, not just to individual team members.

5. *Adjourning Stage—Make acknowledgements, mark progress, and continue relationships beyond.*

Finally, our journey with the team is complete and its life cycle ended.

If I can give you two pieces of advice beyond all this, the first is that you as the leader must let each team member tell their story, including their perspective on how and why they joined the team and their best memory. This will wash away any lingering ill feeling about the storming portions and remind us that this is a group, not a personal project. Secondly, don't say goodbye. Say "till we meet again."

Whether a few team members are leaving or the entire team is being disbanded, you must keep in touch with the departing team members and preserve the relationships built with them, whether they go to a different company, move on to a different department, or retire altogether.

Those relationships and the social capital you have built with them will come in handy for a very long time. The idea is to ensure that this is valued, that people respect it, and that people take advantage of it because this is what will keep professional circles strong for the future when further good work of a similar nature is needed. You will know exactly who to reach out to, the linkages with those people will still be warm, and you'll be able to get the help you need.

How to do this right:

- Emphasize a sense of achievement.
- Reinforce social capital. Don't say goodbye.
- Value individual contributions. Tell stories.

End of the Cycle

So in sum, as a leader taking your team through the journey depicted on Tuckman's model, you are looking to know where your team is at any given point in time, what they need from you, and what must be included in the team meeting for it to get where it needs to go.

Beyond that, maybe you have learned that teams, like people, have a lot of growing up to do. Like young children, new teams can be moody or inconsistent; like adolescents, they can have clashes with those around them; and then at maturity, they finally understand the "big picture" and appreciate everyone who helped them along the way.

And that's enough to make any leader proud.

7

LEADERSHIP STYLE FOR YOUR TEAM

Now that we are learning what leadership is and how we can go about managing our time and relationships, let's try to figure out how we can bring our best style out.

Each personality type and each company culture or situation has different needs in terms of leadership styles.

My approach to leadership is to find the nature or personality of a person and help that person bring out the best of those innate qualities while at the same time molding them into the needs of the culture and situation so that they may achieve the desired result.

For instance, some leaders are natural-born teachers; they ask piercing and insightful questions of their teams and are innately motivated to help them grow in skill level and responsibility. I work with such individuals to ensure they have growth plans for each team member who reports to them (and even some that don't). Others leaders may be excellent at creating compelling visions for their companies or products. I would help such people verbalize and sell their visions to the company and bring a maximum number of people on board.

What's your leadership style? Take a look at the following

statements, each of which describes a different approach to leadership. Which of them do you most agree with?

1. My employees are rusty or new and need a lot of hands-on help.
2. I give my employees freedom, but ultimately I know best.
3. I give my employees a lot of free room to create consensus.
4. My role is primarily vision, top-level authorization, and logistical approvals.
5. I have great employees, and I trust them to do the work.

Naturally, you might choose a combination of two or three of these statements, since each one of us is unique.

In case you were wondering, here is the style of leadership associated with each statement:

1. My employees are rusty or new and need a lot of hands-on help. *(Military General)*
2. I give my employees freedom, but ultimately I know best. *(Project Manager)*
3. I give my employees a lot of free room to create consensus *(Coordinator)*
4. My role is primarily vision, top-level authorization, and logistical approvals. *(Coach)*
5. I have great employees, and I trust them to do the work. *(Mentor)*

Typically, the response I get is a combination of statements 3, 4, and 5. This tells me that leaders have faith in their workers and want them to succeed, but they are aware of the blame (and reward) on the leader's shoulders in the end.

The compromise approach is to at least make sure workers feel that their ideas are heard and that their agreement, as well as consent to decisions, is important to management.

There are so many ways to categorize leaders. Everyone has a unique personality, so naturally each person will be slightly different in their leadership style.

So for the sake of simplicity, let's think of leadership in a handful of ways that vary along this range, from military general (fully autocratic) to mentor (fully democratic).

Have a look at the table below. You'll see a set of five leadership styles, categorized by the following elements:

- ☐ How hands-on the leader is (or should be)
- ☐ How much power the leader has
- ☐ The level of skill the team would possess at this time
- ☐ How experienced the team might be
- ☐ What stage of the (modified) Tuckman's model the team is at

Style	Hands on	Leader Power Level	Team Skill Level	Team Experience Level	Team Phase
Mentor	Least	Least	Maximum	Maximum	Performing
Coordinator	Less	Less	More	More	Performing
Coach	Middle	Middle	Middle	Middle	Storming
Project Manager	More	More	Less	Less	Norming
Military General	Maximum	Maximum	Least	Least	Forming/ Storming

Figure 8. Match your leadership style to your team's stage in the (modified) Tuckman's model.

To simplify matters and to help you visualize better, I renamed the leadership styles according to a real-life role or job that requires this kind of leadership.

✐ Military General

In short, maximum authority for the leader and minimum discretionary power for the team.

This is the approach needed when time is short, risk is high, and the team isn't ready, skilled, or experienced. The leader tells people what to do, how to do it, and when to do it, and there is no time for debate or consensus-making because of the heavy danger ahead. Roles are firm with little room for workers to make their own decisions.

✍ Project Manager

In short, the team is learning, and the leader starts to cut team members some slack.

The team has been doing this work for some time, and the risk isn't overly high, but the workers may still lack the right knowledge or experience, so the leader is still fairly hands on. Some delegation may be possible for low-risk items, roles are more diversified, and there may be the beginnings of a second layer of management.

✍ Coach

In short, now the team really starts to learn the work, but conflict may have to be managed.

Now the team is getting somewhere, they are more knowledgeable and experienced, yet they may be having some amount of "growing pains" during the team cycle phase known as *storming* (see chapter 6 on leading teams). There is probably a certain amount of conflict occurring, and it will take a delicate balance of leadership that encourages and gives orders and yet gives the workers a chance to make decisions and maybe even make some mistakes. The team should be encouraged to discuss and debate ideas, but the coach should retain a sort of veto power to make sure everything stays according to plan.

✍ Coordinator

In short, everyone is getting on the same page. The leader starts to take a step back.

Now the team is at the performing stage. Each member has a clearly defined role and they are united in the vision of the team and have a feeling of unity.

The leader can take a further step back from a hands-on role, and more and more decisions can be delegated to team members.

At this point, the main role of the leader is to give a structure to meetings and planning, keep an eye on progress, and ensure tasks are completed, yet the leader should have faith and trust the workers more than before.

More and more, the leader starts to transform into a mentor.

✐ Mentor

In short, it's not your plan; your team knows what to do.

They've done this before, and they have the skills and experience.

From time to time, they reach out to you for guidance, career advice, and mentorship and to get back to their goals.

The real purpose of the mentor at this stage is to think ahead and find the right use for the leaders that are starting to bloom in the team. The time may be right to plan ahead for them to be moved up a level so they can lead small teams of their own. Then lower members of the team can start to move up.

Everyone gains a level, and the leader can take pride in seeing the vision become a reality.

✐ Which Leadership Style Should I Adopt?

Now comes the hardest part: discovering the optimal leadership style that suits your personality, work circumstances, and team.

Similar to the leadership audit we did in a previous chapter, let's do a team audit.

On a scale of 1 to 5 (1 meaning not at all and 5 meaning perfectly):

a. How well do your team members know their roles?
b. How effective are your team members at sticking to an agenda for a meeting?
c. How proactive are your team members at preventing problems?
d. How confident are you that if a major crisis happened, the team could handle it with minimum input from you?
e. Lastly, can the team effectively present a project status report to your supervisor?

Now average out your scores:

- *4.5 and Above:* You are ready to be a mentor. Watch your team grow with pride and give them valuable feedback and advice to help them move forward.
- *3.9 to 4.4:* You're a coordinator. You'll still need to be fully in the loop, yet there is a lot of room for delegation and discretion. If you're a team of more than ten, definitely consider building a leadership layer between you and the least experienced team members. In fact, this might be worth it even for smaller teams, provided they will be on the project for more than a few months and the team is not expected to grow much. You should always have one "deputy" regardless of the size of the team.
- *3 to 3.9:* You're a coach. Not very hands on, but you will always have the final say. Some conflict still must be managed, but keep working on building that deputy and middle management layer if the team is large enough.
- *2 to 2.9:* You're a project manager. The team is picking it up, but you're still needed at the front lines. You may find an early promise of a "diamond in the rough" to groom into a future leader.
- *Under 2*: You are the general. Take charge because the team is green and the ultimate responsibility is with you.

⟋ Closing Thoughts

A lot more can be said about leadership, and we will certainly have many more conversations about it. But for now it's about having a clear concept of being a leader and the relationship between you and the team; you and the company; and even you and the vision you are pursuing.

It's never been more important to ensure that others have a balanced mix of regard, affection, and respect for your abilities and personality.

They should be willing to trust you and walk with you on the journey. That's the whole point of being a leader.

So how can we make sure of this?

a. *Always make a strong impression.* Leverage a strong but friendly handshake, good eye contact, and a friendly but confident smile.

b. *Show empathy.* Remember people's names and what you were talking about the last time you both met. This shows that you care about them, their well-being, their challenges, and their journey.

c. *Show knowledge as well as growth.* People should respect your knowledge and experience as much as they admire your willingness to keep learning.

d. *Take responsibility.* Give credit to the company and team when they succeed, and take ownership in the losses. The mix of humility and responsibility grows a silent regard for you.

e. *Remember that leadership is communication.* Your leadership style is your message, your rules, and your actions. Be clear with others so they always know what you mean. Be clear with yourself so you are never in doubt. And, if you're not in doubt, you've already won.

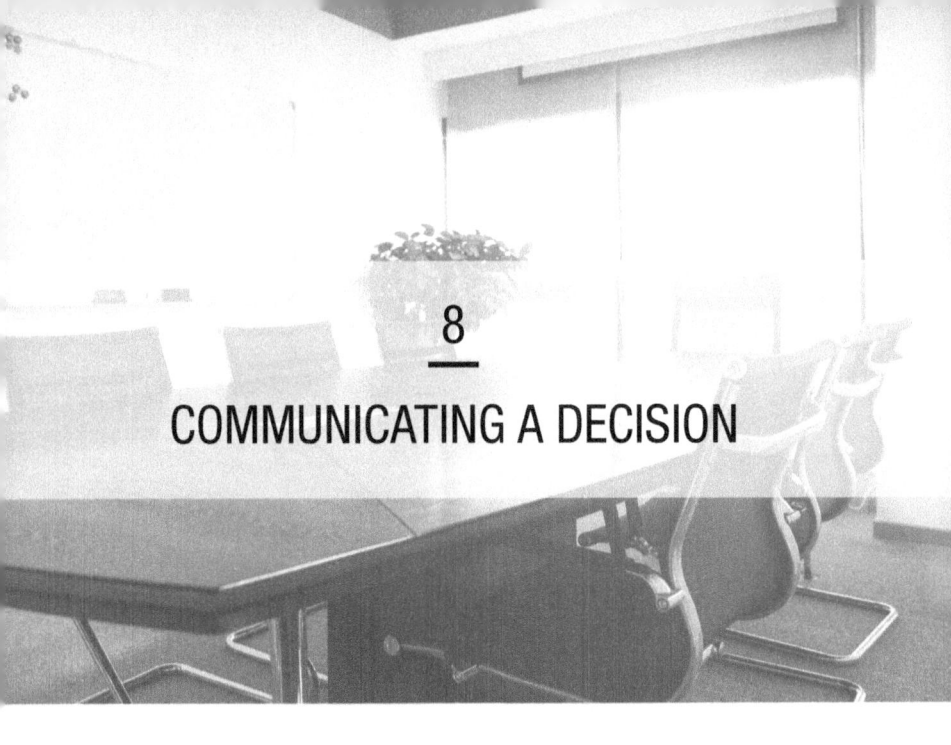

8

COMMUNICATING A DECISION

During the course of your career, you've probably picked up a lot of leadership tips. Maybe you have come across terms like servant leadership14, collaborative leadership, "laisse-faire15," and so on, where the person in charge takes a custodial role but steps back.

That's important to have as an option of strategy, but not all of the time.

To qualify yourself as a person with the qualities to hold your given role, your "fit" for the role has to be substantiated in manners both overt and covert, visible and invisible.

Not to make you hypercompetitive or hypervigilant, but it is no secret that as you rise up in the ranks, colleagues and subordinates are eyeing your position and evaluating your performance.

Worse yet, upper management is constantly seeking "reductions

[14] N. Eva, M. Robin, S. Sendjaya, D. van Dierendonck, and R. C. Liden, "Servant Leadership: A Systematic Review and Call for Future Research," *The Leadership Quarterly* 30, no. 1 (2019): 111–32, https://doi.org/10.1016/j.leaqua.2018.07.004.

[15] Anders Skogstad, Jørn Hetland, Lars Glasø, and Ståle Einarsen, "Is Avoidant Leadership a Root Cause of Subordinate Stress? Longitudinal Relationships between Laissez-Faire Leadership and Role Ambiguity," *Work & Stress* 28, no. 4 (September 2014): 323–41, https://www.tandfonline.com/doi/abs/10.1080/02678373.2014.957362.

in force" to reduce payroll costs and avoid duplications and redundancies.

And if you *are* upper management, you may have a board, shareholders, or investors to worry about.

Most importantly, especially in times of crisis or uncertainty, people need strong presence from those in leadership; they need reassurance that all will be well.

As a leader, at all times, you need to show that

- You mean business,
- You know what you're talking about,
- You deserve to be in charge, and
- Your idea(s) is (are) essential to the path forward.

And all of this because of the clear and essential vision that you present.

We could write many books on leadership (and will), but here are four keys that will jump-start you as a truly communicative leader.

✐ Four Keys to Presentations as a Leader

FOUR KEYS TO BOARD PRESENTATIONS

1. CLEAR DECISION

Firmly but politely tell us
what you have concluded,
and will execute on.

2. PROS AND CONS

Show both sides of the
argument, or at least two
viable options, then tell us
why you picked one of them
over the other.

3. SELL

Drive home your point
Make us agree
Motivate us to follow
through

4. TELL

Cooperation
Sharing Resources
Timeline
Clear roles and responsibilities

Figure 9. Four keys to board presentations

Imagine the decision point of any meeting: Every high-level and microlevel detail has been hashed out. It's now time to clearly state and restate the vision, the plan, and the follow-up and to "pitch" your idea.

It's important to assert yourself clearly as an individual or representative of your team yet find a way to solicit cooperation from others and show connectedness to the organization you're a part of.

You'll want to rehearse this part. Create a slide or cue card with the appropriate bullets. The main goal is to drive home your key points and make them memorably decisive.

Here's a template I've created and have taught my clients. Give it a try!

1. *State your clear decision.*

In a single clear, direct, short, and unambiguous sentence, tell us what you as a leader have decided is the right course of action or policy on a problem. Such sentences reduce equivocation. When needed, they make your values and decision criteria clear. And they become "quotables" to refer to as shorthand for the policy when others are trying to rationalize in their decision-making process. For example, "The customer is always right," is repeated incessantly to remind retailers that having the customer leave with a smile is paramount.

2. *List pros and cons.*

So you've led with your bottom-line decision. Why weigh out pros and cons now? Some of your audience is on the fence, and you need to push them over. If they're on the opposing side, your balanced approach will show that you've "heard them out," yet the decision may well be substantiated in the other direction.

Think of this template as a report: you know the answer and analysis and are just emphasizing the journey up to this point and the journey ahead. The idea of pros and cons is more to show your due diligence and cognizance of all the facts in ample detail.

To close this step, after stating both pros and cons in fair measure and a similar tone of voice, restate the deciding factor that pushed you to your decision. Remember, this is leading up to the next step, the sell.

3. *Sell your decision.*

Now you must persuade the audience of the value of your decision. Let's check at this point: Do you require their conceptual agreement, or do you have them with you conceptually and instead need to enforce compliance?

For both, it is worth restating the benefits of your plan in the short term *and* the long term. For conceptual agreement, you'd need to make unflattering comparisons (but fair ones) with alternative plans, showing yours to be the most robust (e.g., you may make the case that increasing the top line is a better strategy than cost cutting because it increases the company's financial valuation).

For more compliance, you're reemphasizing the long-term benefits (since resistance to change is likely the problem) and offering troubleshooting teams for onboarding any major changes (e.g., new software to be used by employees).

4. *Tell how you'll accomplish it.*

Here's where you tell us what to do and what your next steps are:

a. *Cooperation*: How can others help you in your tasks? Make everyone a part of the process here. Especially for strategic cross-departmental plans, you may not even have a choice. If we aren't "talking to each other," that will increase resistance to the change, so we don't just ask for help; we ask for input and coownership to maximize participation and follow-through.

b. *Sharing resources*: Troubleshooting teams, tech support, and the right combination of hotlines and wikis will ensure everyone can pick your plan up and hit the ground running. Have some items online, and also try to have handouts at the event or meeting to give folks as an easy reference.

c. *Timeline*: What next steps are you going to take? When is each one to be executed? What roles are designated? This is the section in which all large and small details come up and are laid out clearly. Hold yourself as accountable as you hold others so you set the right example. Have smart benchmarks to fairly measure progress. Gantt charts are a great start.

✏️ Sample Template

Not sure how to apply this template to real life? No worries! Here is a sample I threw together. Feel free to adapt it for any of your upcoming meetings.

1. *Decision:* So folks, we are onboarding Recruitr as our new recruitment software.

2. *Pros and cons:* We looked at how it's able to read resumes more quickly and subtly, and there's at least a 10 percent improvement on getting better fit candidates into the interview phase. It's definitely 5 to 7 percent pricier, but we crunched the numbers and the cost will balance out if we can fill out our positions a month or so quicker without reposting the ad.

3. *Sell:* I really think this is so timely with our all-hands meeting where we emphasized it's all about culture with us, and I get the sense Recruitr will give us ready-to-go, awesome people who really sync with our mission and want to be a part of the ride. And really, over time we can ramp up their skills if they're willing to believe in this company and take you folks on as their mentors.

4. *Tell:* I'd love for everyone to do a test drive of the platform and give us your unvarnished opinions and a list of all the bugs. Does it accommodate all our open roles and HR's new application form? I'd love for IT to continue their due diligence, and Matty is working on a great wiki to walk you through the knowledge. She's even making a short two-minute video to give you the tour. The URLs are all posted on that sheet you got, plus there's a PDF in your inbox. Jess is drawing up eight to ten sample resumes with the dummy roles we've created to see what filters through. We've got it to play with until November 10, and I need a final report by November 3 so we can close the contract and get our first role filled with it.

Closing Thoughts

The essence of obtaining agreement from your audience is their confidence that you have reviewed the problem from all viewpoints, "done your homework," found a solution, and mapped out a vision for a successful rollout of the plan. Your clarity, vision, and the finality of your decision are what close the deal, and the forward-thinking plan gets people thinking past it.

Decision, pros and cons, sell, and tell—that's all you have to do to get things done.

9

PLANNING AND RUNNING A MEETING

"Hey, the meeting is cancelled."

Feel disappointed?

Probably not.

More likely you found yourself doing a happy dance in the coffee room.

You might even have said, "Wow. I'll actually get some work done!"

It seems as if meetings became ubiquitous in work life in a very short time, not just as a regular occurrence but also as a performative activity to symbolize work being done. Those who call the meeting demand importance for their roles and ideas, those who participate in the meetings vociferously seem to emphasize their impact on the work environment, and the others play audience in muted agreement of the decisions being made by a few.

With a more recent self-reflection on work culture, companies have started to realize that meetings do not necessarily equal work being done.

So when do meetings become a waste of time?

1.   They're too long.

2. They feel unnecessary (i.e., "this could have been an email").
3. The main discussion gets derailed into side conversations.
4. A few people dominate the conversation, while others get left out.
5. The purpose of the meeting isn't accomplished, so we need another meeting.

It's probably safe to assume that item 4 is the root cause.

Why do a few people end up dominating the whole group's meeting?

This occurs when people are not on the same page; there are unresolved questions and differences of opinion.

If a meeting is not structured or segmented and lacks clear rules of participation, it's easy to see how it can go off the rails and become unproductive, if not entirely harmful, to the group.

Think of meetings as a circle rather than a straight line. Look at this with fresh eyes: each meeting is connected to what happens before the meeting and what occurs after it, leading into the next meeting.

Projects need momentum to succeed, so you need successively productive meetings to ensure that you root out any bugs and resolve issues as they crop up, if not prevent them altogether.

Thus, the ending of one meeting perfectly blends into the beginning of the next meeting.

So let's figure out how to plan for the success of a meeting before it starts, how to execute the meeting itself, and what to do after the meeting is adjourned.

Before the Meeting

1. *Meeting purpose*

If you're the leader, ask yourself: Why do I need to organize this meeting?

One of the issues with meetings is that they are often unnecessary or lack a clear purpose.

So that's your first goal: *prevent unnecessary meetings.*

If all you need to do is provide a report or information to your team, an email is good enough. If they have questions, they can reply or talk with you separately.

Here are some good reasons for organizing a meeting:

a. *Alignment*: Getting on the same page regarding a project or an issue, creating or maintaining team culture, and ironing out differences.

b. *Decision-making*: You have to come up with a course of action to solve a problem, figure out the details of a project, or get the green light and budget from your boss.

c. *Coaching and mentoring:* Things don't have to be misaligned for leaders to meet with subordinates on a one-on-one basis. The best kind of leader is someone who sets periodic meetings to help build team members' skills and grow them into their next roles. This increases their individual capacity and also helps a company plan for the future set of leaders.

Ask yourself: Does the purpose of this meeting fit the purpose of our project(s), the purpose of the team as a whole, and finally *your* purpose as a leader?

Each meeting must move you forward on the chessboard, being part of the strategy, bringing you closer to victory.

The single worst reason for a meeting? "It's on the calendar."

Don't think with the calendar in mind; think with your vision in mind.

Then you can plan your meeting.

2. *Meeting agenda*

You've probably seen an agenda before. It's a list of the items that will be covered in the meeting, ideally with a set order and maybe even a set time for each item to be discussed.

A lot of meetings have items planned out, yet many agenda items get missed, others run over time, and questions are left unanswered, leading to the need for additional meetings.

Let's make sure to plan a smart agenda, which means everything gets done, all questions get answered, everyone knows what they need to do, and we move on to the next step.

There are several types of agenda items:

- *Updates on ongoing items:* Which of your items are purely information being reported? Put those in an email and send it out beforehand. At the beginning of the meeting, recap them in brief and ask if anyone has any questions.
- *Requests for information:* Send agenda items that are simple yes-or-no questions out in an email as well. These days, many companies use instant messaging for these discussions—rapid-fire questions, rapid responses, and we move on to the next item. Think about it. The smart way to avoid long, large-group meetings is to have many small microgroup, micromeetings. Ask a few relevant questions from the key people and move on.
- *Discussion items:* This is where we actually talk to come up with ideas, solve problems, and iron out any questions, differences, and clarifications.
- *Planning:* Next steps, divvying up the work, and so on.
- *Closing items:* These include items to be put on the calendar with deadlines and next steps; follow-up discussions, including one-on-one or small-group meetings (might not require meeting in person); and time for last-minute questions.

3. *Prealignment*

This might not be necessary each time, certainly not for regular meetings or meetings discussing regular items. But once in a while, a problem comes up in which you might be aware that certain key people are disagreeing with the team agenda or the company's decisions.

As the leader, it might be worth your while to briefly check in with those individuals or with each team member after you send out the meeting agenda.

My clients tell me stories about meeting with their counterparts before a big meeting and finding out that said counterparts were slighted or felt bad that their advice was not sought before the decision was made.

A premeeting check-in can make the counterpart(s) felt respected and, despite concerns, willing to come on board with the team decision. This can ensure that the meeting goes off smoothly and all action items are agreed upon.

4. *Logistics*

This is just basic planning for your meeting, a handy checklist for you to run through so you minimize goof ups.

a. *Book a room* large enough for the number of people and for the duration of the meeting (perhaps with time to spare if possible).

b. Ensure the room has the *technology* you need (e.g. internet, audio-visual equipment, and so on).

c. Check and recheck the *email list* of the people you're inviting. Did you leave anyone out by mistake? Could someone else benefit from attending?

d. Use a *calendar software* to make it easy for everyone to confirm participation, and follow up with anyone who doesn't confirm within forty-eight hours of the meeting. Try sending out meeting invites a week before, and if it's a recurring event, then use that setting so you don't have to redo it each time.

e. Is there a file other than the agenda that people should look over? Attach that too. The more *relevant information* you can send beforehand, the better.

✎ During the Meeting

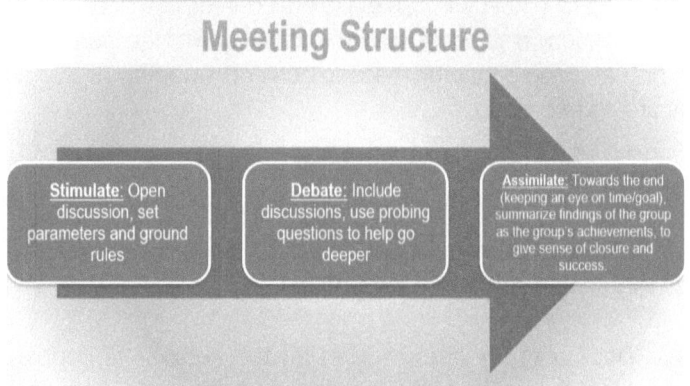

Figure 10. Meeting structure—how to go step-by-step.

Just like a speech, a meeting has an introduction portion, a body portion, and a conclusion.

As the coordinator or key player of the meeting proceedings, it would be wise to plan ahead how the meeting agenda should be discussed. Try to ensure that each item is reasonably well covered and participation is encouraged with an eye on the clock as well as meeting deliverables.

The introduction sets the stage. We will call this the *stimulate* phase. The role of the team leader here is to open the discussion and give everyone the details about the problem or project at hand. Format this as one or more questions. For example, "How can we boost our website's search ranking with the given budget?"

Now you've framed the meeting. It has a purpose.

Make sure you keep the meeting progress closely matched to the purpose.

The next phase is the *debate* phase. Now your job is to get the participation of each attendee and ensure that each participant gets roughly equal speaking time or at least does not leave anything unsaid. If you get this *one* thing right, the meeting will stay on track and on time.

This phase is the problem-solving and brainstorming phase. Many ideas or questions may be thrown around. Keep one eye on the clock to ensure that the problem is explored thoroughly and a good idea or solution is found by the end.

At the minimum, some progress should be made in order to maintain team morale.

The leader's best tool during this phase is to ask moderation questions that do not have judgment. For example, instead of saying, "That doesn't make sense," you might say, "How does that work?"

If during the meeting you feel that someone wants to speak or should speak but is holding back, call that person by name: "Mary, what do you think?"

Finally, remember that you are here to help achieve an objective with the maximum possible inclusive participation. Guide; do not order. Collect and include; do not "quiz."

Rely on supportive communication and declare the "collective goal" at the end.

Expert tip: Use pauses to let everyone speak up. In my experience, I have seen that some very polite people wait up to seven or ten seconds before they will respond.

Some additional tips for the debate phase:

- Ensure that the meeting ends five to ten minutes before the scheduled time. This gives attendees time to breathe before their next meeting, and others can stay behind to ask each other questions and coordinate next steps.
- Ensure there is note-taking during the meeting, ideally using a medium that every attendee can see, be it a whiteboard, blackboard, TV monitor, or shared document that can be viewed on the laptop.
- When you take notes, do not attribute the idea to a particular attendee. This way you collect the *team's* ideas rather than an individual person's ideas. This creates a sense of unity and your group will focus on good ideas rather than making it a competition to gain attention.
- An optional fun tool for large meetings is polling software. You could also use an app or survey website to get responses from the attendees on key questions. This helps the audience stay engaged and gives management valuable feedback.

The last phase, the end of the meeting, is called *assimilate*. This is your chance as the leader to take everything that's been said during the meeting, recap it for all the attendees, assign them their work, and tell them what's happening next.

So you've reached the end of the meeting. Here's a handy checklist of items you'll want to go over with attendees. This will make sure your group leaves the meeting with a feeling of accomplishment, a plan going forward, and exact tasks to be completed.

1. The highlights of the meeting discussion have been recapped.
2. Every agenda item has been addressed (or most of them anyway).
3. Ideas, solutions, and next steps have been planned for the future.
4. Each of these has clear deadlines and follow-ups.
5. Each action has a clear method to measure its effectiveness (e.g., profit numbers, improved satisfaction survey, etc.).
6. Each person has been reminded of their role, tasks, and deadlines.
7. A copy of the agenda and meeting minutes will be sent out to create a record of the meeting and give attendees a feeling of progress.
8. Follow-up individual or small group discussions will be scheduled.
9. Next steps will be turned into agenda prep for next meeting.
10. Dashboard software will be used as a visual real-time progress checker (e.g., Trello). This way each team member is accountable to finish their work on time and with maximum effectiveness.

✍ Closing Thoughts

Even after this discussion, you may find yourself not quite sure at times.

Leaders are constantly having to make judgment calls: Should I hire this person? Should I let this person go? Should we try to fix this project? Should we cancel it?

Deciding whether or not a meeting is required is just another judgment call.

Let's help you make up your mind. Do you agree with any of the following statements?

    a.   This meeting will improve team or individual productivity and/or morale.

    b.   This meeting cannot be summarized in an email.

If A and B are both true, have the meeting. In fact, cancel all other meetings.

If B is false, then use email.

There you have it. Meetings should improve performance, boost morale, and go beyond the ability of email or other media.

Bottom line: if you have a purpose for your meeting, your meeting will have purpose.

10

SHOW CONFIDENCE

We made it. This is the final conversation!

It's been great to talk with you on this journey to better communication and leadership.

We've talked about your fear of speaking or communicating and how that can be overcome by having empathy for your audience and striving to give them the fullest value with your ideas and passion so that you build a strong relationship of trust with them.

Then we learned how to prepare for a speech or speaking situation, using clear structure and a well-planned rehearsal technique, followed by improving our ability to tell great stories and speaking with minimum prep time.

We learned about leadership—what it is, what it isn't, how it binds and energizes teams, and how our leadership style adapts to the team and its stage of development.

Finally, we learned how to apply our leadership and communication skills with powerful, persuasive presentations and running highly productive meetings.

What else could there possibly be to talk about?

✐ The "X" Factor

We have all met someone like this—people who can walk into a room and command attention without any visible effort, be liked by others, and always have great impact on those around them.

You already know how to be a smart speaker and leader. Now let's put the cherry on top with a collection of small techniques we can practice—techniques that by themselves don't make much impact but, put together and done consistently, create an aura of importance around us.

In short, let's learn five simple ways to show confidence and be taken seriously by others.

1. *The eyes have it*

You can hear someone advise you a thousand times to "make eye contact" during a speaking situation, yet most people either avoid eye contact or keep it to a minimum. This is because we are confronted with the most powerful problem, going back to chapter one: our fear of public speaking situations and, specifically, the "public" part of it. We're worried about losing our rhythm by looking into someone's eyes and going off track. And there's the ever-present fear of judgment.

Let's try to first rationalize the benefit. Why make eye contact? Why not look down at your note cards or stare at a computer screen throughout?

Studies[16] show that when you make eye contact with your audience, not only do they start to pay attention more, but they are instantly engaged almost in a personal conversation with you and add a positive evaluation to the content of your discussion. In simple terms, if you make eye contact with someone while you're speaking, this courageous act on your part makes that person trust you, like you, and maybe even agree with you. If you're in sales, you'll sell more. If you're an educator, students will attend class more and do their homework diligently. If you are a politician, you'll get voted in.

---

[16] Jari K. Hietanen, "Affective Eye Contact: An Integrative Review," *Frontiers in Psychology* 9 (August 2018): 1587, https://doi.org/10.3389/fpsyg.2018.01587.

All because you took the time to look into the audience member's eyes.

You may be wondering, how can I look in everyone's eyes? There might be up to twenty or even one hundred people in the room.

Here's a trick or two to try. If you're in a typical lecture room that's rectangular with rows of chairs, find the person farthest on the left, the person farthest from you on the right, and a person somewhere in the middle. Then, while speaking, oscillate like a fan from left to center, center to right, and then back in the other direction. Do this every minute of your speech.

Nervous? Look at people's hairlines instead of their eyes and still go left to right. It's OK to ease yourself into the habit, and when you see that the sky didn't fall, you can take slightly more risk each time. Find a couple of friendly faces in the room and focus on them next. Then add more such faces. Before you know it, you'll be able to look at anyone.

Here's the key: you avoid reading from your notes or screen as much as possible, and you turn your body left to right and back. And at a minimum, the audience at least *feels* like you're giving them eye contact, even if you're not directly looking at them (initially, when nervous).

This shouldn't even need to be said, but *never* read from a phone or tablet. Unless you want to give away all your gravitas.

Eye contact is a mutual act. You look at them, they look at you, and you'll both *see* each other.

2. *Head, shoulders, knees, and toes*

It's a point we tend to forget, but posture, body language, and body positioning are critical to being respected, and the remedies are remarkably simple adjustments.

Start by ensuring your stance is as straight and sure as possible. This is to show strength in every sense of the word. A straight back with level shoulders and no slouching shows that you are ready for the situation and focused on the job at hand.

Keeping your knees extended and feet as far apart as your shoulders gives you good balance and the ability to adapt quickly with your movements. Your toes should point forward rather than in or out.

Finally, what do you do with your hands?

Simple stuff: avoid putting them in your pockets or crossing your arms. Hands in pockets connote an overly causal approach, and crossing your arms shows defiance, lack of open mindedness, or even aggression.

Hand motions while speaking are quite critical. Find the right speed and momentum. A trick you can use is to make one hand your utility hand; it's the one you use to hold notes, a PowerPoint slide clicker, your microphone, or any other implement. If you don't need to hold anything, well you're in luck!

Make your other hand your gesturing hand. Use gentle, open-handed movements (flat palm, no pointing fingers, held outward) in a wavy motion at the same speed that you're talking.

Any time you call out a number—"There are three ways to …"—motion that number with your hand (e.g., hold up three fingers).

If you have the room to walk around, mark the floor center and walk no more than three steps to your left, turn on your feet, walk back to the center mark on the stage or floor, take no more than three steps to your right, and then go back to the center.

In short, gentle hand movements with some gestures and a straight and firm back, shoulders, and feet.

3. *Speak like you're singing*

Tone means everything when we're speaking.

Try it. Say it flat: "How are you?"

Now add emphasis and inflection: "How ARE *you*?"

Especially if you add an upward inflection in the "you," the second option seems more engaged and perhaps more sincere.

Think about any one sentence of your speech or conversation and break it into two parts. For example, "The cow jumped over the moon." The two parts are "the cow jumped" and "over the moon."

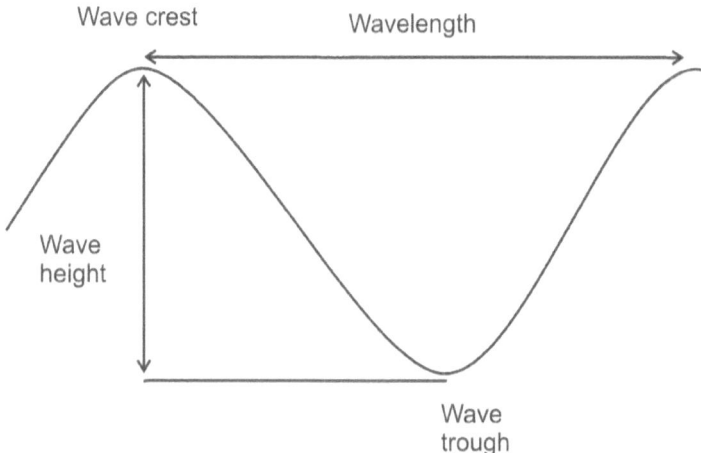

Figure 11. Structure of a sound wave form
with two crests and two troughs

So let's say it this way: "The COW jumped OVER the moon."
See what we did?

We heightened the tone of the words *cow* and *over* (only slightly) and maintained the other words' level. So like in the diagram, we created two crests of the wave, or two high points, and two troughs, or low points. Longer sentences may have more than two pairs of crests and troughs.

This is called prosody[17], and it shows that when we add tonal variation to our language, we are able to communicate at a higher level, called paralanguage, and this adds to the meaning and pleasantness of the words we speak.

Simply put: it's like singing. Create a melody with your words so people will want to listen.

4. *Simple message*

In reading this book, you may have noticed something: There were very few words present that the average person would have to look up in a dictionary. Yet there's more than a little useful information here.

---

[17] Frank Boutsen, "Prosody: The Music of Language and Speech," *The ASHA Leader* (March 1, 2003), https://doi.org/10.1044/leader.FTR1.08042003.6.

That's true communication, reaching the largest possible audience without compromising the message.

Simple messages are the most profound.

How do we simplify our message?

a. Use short sentences.
b. Make use of lists to organize steps or components in some order (e.g., a timeline).
c. Use templates like in chapter 8. Tell us right up top what the talk is about, and *then* go about elaborating on it. Simple structures, predictable formats—they all promote memory.
d. Preview in the beginning, and summarize at the end. Always remind your audience what you talked about. Always ask yourself: What's the *one* thing I want them to remember? Make sure you say that at least twice, once in the beginning and once toward the end.
e. Ask two to three questions during a speech or talk. It engages your audience, gets them thinking, and acts as a great transition point to the next item.
f. Use standout words carefully. Should you use advanced vocabulary? Sparingly, for impact. Same goes for slang. More than a couple of instances and it loses its meaning.
g. Avoid split infinitives or any other dilutions. For example, instead of saying, "I'm not entirely sure," say, "I'm unsure."
h. Keep word count and time under par. An email doesn't need to be longer than three hundred words. Most speeches or talks should be two to five minutes long. And always have the two-minute version ready when a busy executive comes by.
i. Use active voice rather than passive voice. Say "I'm doing X" instead of "X is being done" (most of the time, anyway). Active speech shows leadership; passive speech shows togetherness and can be used to deescalate situations.

5. *Inspire, motivate, humanize*

You may be wondering how in the world "inspiring" someone is a simple technique.
It's actually quite straightforward.

You can accomplish it with a four-part technique:

1. I know you.
2. I believe in you.
3. I'm here for you.
4. It's going to be fine.

We talk about so many ideas, sometimes very deep topics only people with our level of expertise can understand. Yet everyone we talk to is a person, and so are we.
People always need other people. There's just no way around that.
We need other people to know who we are, to care about us, to recognize our efforts, to cheer us on in tough times, to congratulate us when we do well, and to encourage us when things don't go our way.
Optimism, acknowledgment, and encouragement are your superpowers as a communicator and leader.
If you can find an authentic way—simple, *personalized* language that shows you have been paying attention to the other person, that you remember their past deeds and that you see a bright future—to convey this, they will follow you to the ends of the earth.
Try something like this: "You know, I can't imagine what you're going through. This is really good work, really tough luck that it didn't go your way. I see your effort. I know you're trying your best. Let's keep talking. You're not alone, and we'll walk every step of the way. You'll get there."
If you don't give up on them, they won't give up either.

✍ In Closing

People, clients, and friends always ask me, "How do you know what to say in any given situation?"

It's true that, for all our prep, rehearsal, talent, and endless effort, life keeps throwing something new at us, something we maybe couldn't have predicted.

The solution is simple:

- ➲ Be brave.
- ➲ Be truthful.
- ➲ Be compassionate.

Do these three things and you'll always know what to say.

Get the feeling right and the words will follow.

Remember: words are just sounds that mean something and give us a certain feeling.

So let's make some sounds that most people understand and find important and that make them feel good. And then maybe they'll make some sounds back that appeal to others. Thus, the cycle continues.

That's the recipe for creating a great community. Lots of good and interesting talking … together.

Bibliography

Boutsen, Frank. "Prosody: The Music of Language and Speech." *The ASHA Leader* (March 1, 2003). https://doi.org/10.1044/leader.FTR1.08042003.6.

Boyes, Alice. "What Is Catastrophizing?" *In Practice* (blog). *Psychology Today*. January 10, 2013. https://www.psychologytoday.com/us/blog/in-practice/201301/what-is-catastrophizing-cognitive-distortions.

Brewer, Geoffrey. "Snakes Top List of Americans' Fears." *Gallup News Service*, March 19, 2001. https://news.gallup.com/poll/1891/snakes-top-list-americans-fears.aspx.

Hietanen, Jari K. "Affective Eye Contact: An Integrative Review." *Frontiers in Psychology* 9 (August 2018). https://doi.org/10.3389/fpsyg.2018.01587.

Markus, Hazel. R., and Shinobu Kitayama. "The Cultural Shaping of Emotion: A Conceptual Framework." In *Emotion and Culture: Empirical Studies of Mutual Influence*, edited by S. Kitayama and H. R. Markus, 339–51. American Psychological Association. Accessed March 21, 2021. https://doi.org/10.1037/10152-020.

Monroe, Alan H. *Principles and Types of Speech.* 5th ed. Chicago: Scott Foresman, 1962.

Nathan, Eva, Mulyadi Robin, S. Sendjaya, Dirk van Dierendonck, and Robert. C. Liden. "Servant Leadership: A Systematic Review and Call for Future Research." *The Leadership Quarterly* 30, no. 1 (February 2019): 111–32. https://doi.org/10.1016/j.leaqua.2018.07.004.

Nordquist, Richard. "Exigence in Rhetoric." *Thoughtco*, 2019. https://www.thoughtco.com/exigence-rhetoric-term-1690688.

Pulakos, Ed, and Neall Schmitt. "Experience-Based and Situational Interview Questions: Studies of Validity." *Personnel Psychology* 48 (May 1995): 289–308.

Sestric, Lia. "The Most Profitable 'As Seen on TV' Products of All Time." *Yahoo! Finance*, August 26, 2019. https://finance.yahoo.com/news/most-profitable-seen-tv-products-090000530.html.

Skogstad, Anders, Jørn Hetland, Lars Glasø, and Ståle Einarsen. "Is Avoidant Leadership a Root Cause of Subordinate Stress? Longitudinal Relationships between Laissez-Faire Leadership and Role Ambiguity." *Work & Stress* 28, no. 4 (September 2014), 323–41. https://www.tandfonline.com/doi/abs/10.1080/026783 73.2014.957362.

Stossel, Scott "The Man Who Counts the Killings." *The Atlantic*, May 1997. https:// www.theatlantic.com/magazine/archive/1997/05/the-man-who-counts-the-killings/376850/.

Tuckman, Bruce W. "Developmental Sequence in Small Groups." *Psychological Bulletin* 63, no. 6 (June 1965): 384–99. https://doi.org/10.1037/h0022100.

Walsh, Dylan. "Rethinking Hierarchy in the Workplace." *Insights by Stanford Business*, September 5, 2017. https://www.gsb.stanford.edu/insights/rethinking-hierarchy-workplace.

About the Author

Arjun Buxi is an executive coach to Silicon Valley Tech Company Leaders, a university lecturer in communication and leadership, and an award-winning collegiate debater. He has spent ten years training and teaching others how to improve communication and leadership skills. He earned a master's degree in communication and bachelor's degrees in business and communication. He brings a lifelong experience of being part of family-owned businesses and helping students and entrepreneurs alike find their voice.

Index

V

www.ingramcontent.com/pod-product-compliance
Lightning Source LLC
Chambersburg PA
CBHW021445210526
45463CB00002B/637